BLUE COAT : GREY

Blue Coat Boy in Sunday Dress 1905.

BLUE COAT : GREY COAT

The Blue & Grey Coat Schools and
St Stephen's Home of York
1705 - 1983

W. B. Taylor B.A., M.Phil.

Sessions Book Trust
York, England

© 1997 W. B. Taylor

ISBN 1 85072 188 2

Printed in 11 on 12½ point Plantin Typeface
from Author's disk
by Sessions of York
The Ebor Press
York, England

Contents

Chapter		Page
	Illustrations	vi
	Foreword	vii
	Introduction	viii

A. THE BLUE COAT SCHOOL 1705-1947
I	1705-1863: A rudimentary chance in life	1
II	1863-1927: A progressive headmaster arrives	18
III	1927-1947: Heyday and closure	36

B. THE GREY COAT SCHOOL 1705-1983
IV	1705-1783: High hopes followed by child labour	47
V	1783-1850: A major reform by the ladies	52
VI	1850-1921: The gradual refinement of Victorian values	60
VII	1921-1945: The reluctant introduction of co-education	72
VIII	1945-1983: A merger and a change of emphasis	81

C. ST STEPHEN'S HOME 1870-1969
IX	1870-1919: A worthy private charity is born	95
X	1919-1945: A new home	105
XI	1945-1969: A final change of role	117
	Epilogue	128
	Trustees of the York Children's Trust 1996	129
	Bibliography	130
	Illustration Acknowledgements	131
	Index of People Mentioned	132

Illustrations

	Page
Commemorative Plaque 1996 by Dick Reid ...	... *Front cover*
Blue Coat Boy in Sunday Dress 1905	...*Frontispiece*
St Anthony's Hall	2
Interior of St Anthony's Hall as a schoolroom...	3
'South East View of York' by Henry Cave 1816	11
Edward Robinson, Headmaster 1863-1892	19
Old Blue Coat Scholars 1905 (some with their wives) ...	25
Old Grey Coat Scholars 1905 (some with their husbands)...	26
Cecil T.B. Amos, Headmaster 1927-1946	37
Front entrance, Grey Coat Schoool, Monkgate	50
Mrs Catherine Cappe 1744-1821	53
Miss Bazzard with girls in traditional dress	74
Dr W.A. Evelyn 1860-1935	102
25 Trinity Lane	106
69 The Mount (by Alfred Gill)	106
Miss Marshall (centre) and her charges...	111
Blue Coat window – St Helen's Church	... *Back cover*

Foreword

THE YEAR 2005 WILL MARK three centuries since the foundation of the Blue and Grey Coat Schools and 135 years from the beginning of St Stephen's Orphanage.

This book has been commissioned by the York Children's Trust not only as a valuable historical document but also as a tribute to all the hundreds of concerned and caring people who have tried to improve the lot of thousands of young people in the City of York over the last three hundred years.

It is hoped it will be of interest not only to members of the general public but particularly so to descendants of those who attended the three institutions.

Following the closure of the Blue Coat School in 1947, and the amalgamation of the Grey Coat School with St Stephen's Home in 1969, the York Children's Trust was formed in 1976. Since that time the Committee of the Trust has helped many hundreds of young people, up to the age of 24 years, in innumerable ways where adequate help is not available from local authority or government sources.

The publication of this book has been made possible as a result of generous support given by the Sessions Book Trust, for which the Committee is extremely grateful.

JACK P. BIRCH
Chairman, York Children's Trust

Introduction

IN THE SUMMER OF 1705 Annabella Newham took up her responsibilities as the first Matron of the Blue Coat School for boys in St Anthony's Hall. Coincidentally the archives of this school, and of the Grey Coat School for girls, are stored in the same building – now called the Borthwick Institute.

The surviving minutes of the Blue Coat and Grey Coat Schools, known collectively as the Charity Schools, cover almost all their long span of existence. These sometimes parallel sets of minutes, extending over 205 years, form the core of this record of their history. Annual reports and press items provide additional information. This account is followed by the story of St Stephen's Home, the third of the organisations which were the forerunners of the York Children's Trust. The archives of St Stephen's are also preserved at the Borthwick Institute.

Minutes tend to be unemotional summaries of discussions prepared by secretaries who are not necessarily wordsmiths and who do not summarise the arguments for or against a particular committee decision – or the strength of feelings displayed in arriving at those decisions.

Nevertheless a number of important issues emerge from the archives. The high calibre of the current headmaster, headmistress or matron was the common factor in the several particularly successful periods in the life spans of the three institutions – when measured by the quality of life of the resident children. There were clearly many occasions when the male and female members of the voluntary committees were at odds with each other regarding the manner in which the institutions should be run. A major concern early this century was the timing of the inevitable change from in-house education to attendance at state schools. There were also opposing views regarding the continuation, or closure, of the institutions themselves.

Any student of local historical events leans heavily on the excellent library services available in York. I record my gratitude to the staffs at the Borthwick Institute and York Reference Library for their willing assistance and cooperation. I am particularly indebted to a number of Old Scholars who provided me with accounts of life in the schools and home, in some cases in response to a letter kindly published by *The Yorkshire Evening Press*. The notes provided by Mrs Dorothy Brown concerning life at the Grey Coat School and by Mrs Monica Leak for St Stephen's were particularly valuable. Many other informants generously contributed items to fit into the jigsaw.

I have received much help and encouragement from Mr J.P. Birch, Chairman of the York Children's Trust, and from Mr W.K. Sessions, Chairman of the Sessions Book Trust. Richard York and the team at the Ebor Press brought the project to fruition.

Shepherd Homes spontaneously provided documentation and photographs covering the earlier history of St Stephen's. Sir Marcus Worsley Bt. kindly suggested the inclusion of the pencil drawing of St Stephen's Home by Alfred Gill and commented on the chapters dealing with St Stephen's Home.

Finally I owe a debt of gratitude to my wife, Ruth, my friend, Keith Scott, and a number of other readers for each casting a keen eye over the draft manuscript.

W.B. TAYLOR

A. THE BLUE COAT SCHOOL
1705-1947

CHAPTER I
1705-1863
A rudimentary chance in life

THE FOUNDING of the residential Blue Coat School for boys by York Corporation on Thursday 14 June 1705, in the year the French were defeated at Blenheim by the Duke of Marlborough, was probably the most important event in the eighteenth century in the field of education in the City. The name Blue Coat comes from the long blue coat, girded at the loins with a leather belt, which was worn by the pupils of Christ's Hospital in London, an institution founded by Edward VI in the year of his death.

The York school was a local response to the Charity School movement which swept the country in the reign of Queen Anne as part of the national religious revival following a period of political and religious unrest. At that time there was no state provision for the education of children of the poor. The movement was begun by non-conformists and spread to the much larger Church of England where the main purpose was to educate such children in reading, writing, moral discipline and the principles of the Church. The initiative, which was particularly strong between 1696 and 1714, was also designed to protect children from vagrancy and provide them with limited training to fit them for menial service.

A leading figure in the movement at national level was Robert Nelson (1656-1715), a beneficed clergyman and a founder of the

St Anthony's Hall.

SPCK, who refused to take the oath of allegiance to William and Mary. He was a popular writer of works on devotional subjects, and a propagandist of the merits of Charity Schools, who conducted an extensive correspondence on the subject with Church leaders and other influential men throughout the country. There is no direct evidence of his involvement with the founders of the Blue Coat School in York nor is there any indication of a link between the Blue Coat School in York and either Christ's Hospital or any of the other 80 or 90 Blue Coat schools which existed in England at one time or another. Nevertheless most of these schools maintained an eye-catching local profile by means of civic processions, founders' day and civic services, and the wearing of uniforms when out on the streets, all with the object of attracting financial support from the general public.

The local promoters included the Archbishop of York Dr John Sharp, the Dean The Hon. Reverend Henry Finch, Robert Sharp an Alderman and M.P. together with the Lord Mayor, Charles Redman who was described as being particularly zealous in attending preparatory meetings and in securing annual subscriptions amounting to £190. The close continuing support of the

Interior of St Anthony's Hall as a schoolroom.

school by the Corporation in the years to come ensured that the school, unlike other local educational establishments, was a continuing success story throughout the century.

Lady Hewley gave a donation of £400 divided between the boys' school and the Grey Coat School for girls, the Lord Mayor and Commonalty of York gave £100, supplemented by a subscription of £10 a year, and the Ladies of the Thursday Assembly donated £40. The Archbishop and the Dean gave £10 each, Lord Bingley gave £250 and Alderman Robert Fairfax gave £50. It was decided by the ruling committee that a list of benefactors should be set up in the Guildhall, an indication of the civic status of the School.

The School opened in St Anthony's Hall, a building erected in 1450 on the site of St Martin's chapel which was built in 1271. The Hall was constructed for the Guild of St Anthony which entertained Henry VIII and Catherine Howard in the building in 1541. This Guild was spared the general suppression of charities in 1545 and was finally dissolved in 1627 when the Master and keepers delivered up their symbols to the Lord Mayor. Other lesser guilds also used the building and in 1623 forty nine of the Guilds of the City contributed to its repair. The Hall was later utilised for a remarkable variety of purposes including a poor house, weaving factory, Corporation corn mill, armoury, war magazine and archery court. The premises were converted to a hospital and storehouse during both the Civil War and the Great Plague, and then became a House of Correction.

Part of the building was modified at a cost of £150 and taken over by the Blue Coat school in 1705, alongside the House of Correction. The Great Hall was divided into three parts, with one outside aisle acting as a dormitory where the forty boys slept two to a bed. The other outside aisle was reserved for eating and schooling and the centre aisle was used as a workroom.

The institution provided board and lodgings, clothing and tuition for orphans and children of poor families with the children of freemen receiving preference. Entrants were confined primarily to those belonging to the City of York and the immediate neighbourhood. For most of the eighteenth century upwards of 10% of the boys of York passed through the school. This proportion declined in the nineteenth century when the facilities of the school did not keep pace with the increase in the population of York.

Parents or guardians were required to relinquish control and management of a child during its residence at the school and to concede the authority to place the child to trade or service. Parents or guardians who removed children without permission incurred a fine of forty shillings. This penalty was increased to £10 in 1760 and a man was imprisoned in the following year for failing to pay the penalty.

Admission to vacant places was by means of a quarterly ballot amongst supporters of the school, also known as subscribers or directors, who paid annual subscriptions of at least 10 shillings. This contribution entitled them at each ballot to assign one vote to a boy candidate, and a further vote to a girl candidate for the Grey Coat School. In the next century subscribers of one guinea were entitled to two votes and an annual subscription of three guineas carried a three vote entitlement. The multiple votes were confined to one male, and one female, candidate at each election. Donors of £10 received one vote and a £25 donation carried a two vote entitlement. One executor of any person bequeathing of a legacy of £100 upwards was also entitled to one vote. Hence some York solicitors carried several votes including votes for any personal subscriptions or donations.

The numbers of candidates for each vacancy varied from a handful to a high figure of 22 in 1826. On that occasion the successful entrant for the sole vacant place was the son of Kilvington, a poor wireworker who had been killed by lightning the previous summer. Nearly two hundred years later one of his descendants tendered for snow guards for the roof of the school.

The boys were expected to work within the school from the minimum age at entry of 7 years until they reached 12 years of age when they were put as apprentices to sea, or to some mechanical trade, or into domestic service. When a boy was ready to leave the school the Parish Officers of his parish of settlement were required to find an employer for the lad, failing which he would be turned adrift.

In the early days it was intended that the boys should serve in ships of war and three boys joined the 'Shrewsbury' under Captain Palliser in 1758. Other boys were apprenticed to merchant ships, including a boy who was apprenticed to Captain Jefferson of the Contract Fleet which carried wholesale butter in barrels between York and London. In 1778 a shipowner from Scarborough took six boys between the ages of 10 and 15 for sea service and mariners from Staithes and from Hull took other boys for similar work. Seagoing apprenticeships in the Merchant Navy continued until the 1850s.

The boys apprenticed locally were accorded the same status by the Guilds as freemen's sons and were therefore eligible to gain their freedom by patrimony. This concession enabled the boys - at the age of 21 - to qualify for their freedom, and hence a Parliamentary vote, without necessarily completing an apprenticeship. In 1775 a boy was apprenticed to Thomas Haxby of Blake Street, then described as a musician but better known as maker of musical instruments. Another boy was apprenticed in 1780, at the age of 13 years, in the trade of a surgeon. His seven year period of servitude was spent with an apothecary, one of the more highly skilled trades, for which the apprenticeship premium in York was normally £20. Masters were required to provide their apprentices with clothes and necessaries, together with a new suit of clothes to the value of £4, at the end of their apprenticeships. Most local guilds operated rules which restricted the numbers of apprentices who could be employed by each master at any one time, a constraint which arguably impeded the expansion of economic activity in York in the eighteenth century.

In order to extend the range of benefactors the School broadened its intake to children of non-freemen including 'those who have most children and least to maintain them with' or 'parents over-burdened with children'. These parents, or parish officers from townships outside York, were required to pay forty shillings at the outset to purchase clothes for their children in their first year in the school. In different periods in the history of the school the age of entry of individual pupils varied between 7 and 10 years and the age of leaving ranged between 12 and 16 years.

The pupils undertook industrial work with the dual objectives of inuring the children to labour and helping towards the running expenses of the institution. They worked at spinning and weaving for three hours each morning and for three and a half hours in summer afternoons, reduced to one and a half hours in the remainder of the year. The boys were also taught to knit for one hour each Holy Day. The spinning of yarn for serges and shalloons (bed covers) was mostly undertaken for contractors who, in the early days, paid the school £8 per annum for the output of the boys, a figure which had risen to £81 in 1781 and fallen to £36 by 1804. The Committee paid the Spinning Mistress, Catherine Thompson, £8 a month towards the maintenance of the boys with an additional sum of £8 per quarter allowed to her for fire (coal and turf), candles and stockings.

The turning of hardwoods to produce trinkets known as 'toys' was introduced into the curriculum in 1778 and six boys at a time went to a workshop in Goodramgate to learn this trade which was a minor local industry.

Holidays, feast and fast days and attendance at Church accounted for 78 days of the year in the early period of the school. By 1762 the number of such breaks from normal routine had increased to 130 days a year, including attendance at the Minster on Holy Days. The children returned to their parents or guardians during school holidays.

For more than 100 years industrial training took precedence over moral and intellectual training with the result that the boys were educated for a total of only about an hour a day. During this comparatively brief period of daily tuition in groups of ten they were taught to read, write and cast accounts and were instructed in the principles of the Church of England. On leaving the school the boys were fitted out with a suit of clothes and given a Bible and a Book of Common Prayer. Each boy received continuing assistance from the school throughout his subsequent period of servitude, which was completed successfully by about half of those bound apprentice. Old pupils who could produce a certificate of good character were given more books after three years into their apprenticeship and boys who completed their period of servitude to the satisfaction of the Governors received a gift of thirty shillings and were called 'School apprentices'. Leavers who were bound apprentice, and found clothes and necessaries at the expense of the Parish, were known as 'Charity apprentices'.

The boys were clothed in coats faced and trimmed with yellow, sand coloured waistcoats, leather breeches worn without braces, grey stockings and round bonnets which cost a total of 26 shillings. They were required to wear this uniform when abroad in the City so that their benefactors could observe their behaviour. They also paraded in these uniforms, with other organisations, on festive and commemorative occasions such as the formal opening of Lendal Bridge in January 1863.

In 1711 a tailor charged £5 for making 40 pairs of breeches, £2 for making, facing and trimming 40 waistcoats, and 9 shillings for making, facing and trimming four coats. A shoemaker and translator (cobbler) was appointed in 1771 to make, and keep in good repair, two pairs of shoes per annum for each of the 50 boys then in the School. A third pair apiece was introduced some years later.

In the middle of the century the tailor was ordered to make an additional 30 pairs of leather breeches to improve the neatness and tidiness of the boys. Ground lamb leather was sought for the boys' breeches in place of alum leather which 'in cloudy weather is very damp and prejudicial to the thighs and knees of the boys'.

The daily meals cost a halfpenny per head and consisted of milk or milk pottage for breakfast, and broth with a piece of bread for supper. The midday dinner was vegetable-based, including pease pudding. Meat was served on Sundays and Thursdays. Brown wheaten bread replaced the less palatable black oat, rye or barley bread in the 1750s. The children ate off communal pewter plates which were replaced by wooden trenchers in 1781 at 3s.6d. per dozen and finally, in 1848, by individual plates. After one hundred years of evening darkness candles were introduced in 1805. From the 1770s onwards about half the cost of feeding the boys was met out of the income accruing from a legacy of £9,243 bequeathed to the school by William Haughton, an eccentric dancing master and past Sheriff of York.

The management of the schools was in the hands of a committee of subscribers together with a Master, Joseph Beckett, who was appointed to this position in 1712 in order to reinforce the supervision of the boys and raise the low moral tone. He and Mrs Annabella Newham, who served as the first matron from the opening of the school in 1705, both continued in office until 1725. Mrs Newham was allowed 40 shillings a year for a maid to assist with keeping the boys clean, combing their heads and making their beds. In 1714 matron requested a loan of £5 from the Committee until Lammas to meet the high cost of wheat to feed her own cows. The latter would provide fresh milk for the boys for breakfast and for puddings. It was recorded four years later that if she made any increased demands for financial assistance in caring for the 40 boys she should be dismissed.

The administrative affairs of the School were dealt with by a Steward and Treasurer, Timothy Mortimer, who was paid £4 per annum. He was succeeded by his son, also Timothy Mortimer, in 1750 and the management of the affairs of the two Charity Schools was simplified when the funds of both were merged into one account.

In 1710 a bill was received by the School for medical expenses. The items listed were ointment for heads, brimstone, and bags for curing ague together with the fees for bathing in Lady Well on the New Walk. Three boys were touched for the evil in 1714, a proceedings which cost two shillings for nine white loaves and nine pints of ale. Francis Drake, the historian, became the surgeon to the School in 1736.

The mistress of the School offended the Committee in some way in 1752 because her request to purchase a new style washing machine was deferred until the next quarterly meeting when she acknowledged her unspecified misbehaviour. It was stipulated that the equipment could only be used for the benefit of the School.

A link with the American War of Independence became evident in 1783 when William, the son of Joshua Stewart, was admitted. His father had been killed some years earlier in the 'Countess of Scarborough' in a naval engagement with John Paul Jones.

The school possessed no foundation fund or endowment and the early income of the school was derived from the voluntary subscriptions of clergy, gentry and citizens. In subsequent years the income was augmented by bequests, interest on investments and annual benefit plays at the Theatre Royal. The boys were on occasion paraded through the streets to drum up support for the plays at the theatre. It seems that in 1788 that the loss in revenue incurred by Tate Wilkinson, the Master of the Theatre Royal, in giving a charity performance for the benefit of the Schools and the County Hospital was causing great hardship for this benefactor. The Committee agreed to relinquish the benefit and encourage Wilkinson to become an annual subscriber.

It soon became apparent that it was necessary to undertake periodic drives to obtain new subscribers to replace those who had died or dropped out. In 1778, after a twelve year lapse in recruitment, clergymen were requested to seek further donors amongst their parishioners. They were reminded that boys were only accepted into the School from parishes outside York if there was support for the School, in the form of subscribers, from such parishes.

The Committee embarked on a policy of land acquisition in the middle of the eighteenth century to provide rental income, beginning with arable fields purchased at Riccall in 1750. Other agricultural holdings, were purchased at Foston (farm); Tadcaster (homestead and land); Knapton (dairy farm); Lundus Green near Pannal (dairy farm); Murton (dairy farm); Riccall (more arable fields); Holtby (arable fields); and a house with a garden at Monkgate. There were many minor disposals and additions over the years and the total holdings amounted to nearly 500 acres under the supervision of the steward and an Estates sub-committee. A farm at Foston continues to this day to bear the name 'Blue Coat Farm'.

The funds of the Blue Coat School began to accumulate from legacies in the 1770s and surplus funds were put out at interest with private individuals and with such bodies as the Commissioners of Sherburn Inclosure. The total amount put out was about £1,600 of which £600 was placed with Lord Fauconberg. These loans were called in by 1780. The funds of the school were augmented substantially some forty years later when a legacy of £4,000 was received from Thomas Wilkinson, a one-time alderman of York.

In an unusual fund raising venture in 1816 Henry Cave published a print of a South East view of York for the benefit of the two Charity Schools. Cave was a drawing master at the Manor School and a talented engraver and oils and water colour artist.

The church collection at an annual charity sermon, preached originally on St Thomas's Day, was devoted to the school. For much of the century the service was held on Good Friday - apart from an unsuccessful experimental switch to Ash Wednesday in the 1750s. The first sermon, preached in 1706, was printed in London for Francis Hildyard, a York bookseller. Archbishop Herring spoke at four Annual Services and was well supported in the offertory boxes. Laurence Sterne, author of 'Tristram Shandy' preached the sermon in 1747 and the collection was £64. When the famous wit, the Reverend Sydney Smith, provided the charity sermon in 1810 a record collection of £111 was taken, equivalent to nearly £7,000 in today's values. The average annual sum donated at the 85 church collections in the eighteenth century was £68 17s. 6d equivalent to about £4,000 in modern money, an indication of the

'South East View of York' by Henry Cave, 1816.

remarkable spirit of generosity displayed by members of the congregations towards the Charity Schools. In the early years some of the annual services were held in the Minster, a venue which was changed subsequently to St Michael-le-Belfrey.

The children of the two charity schools attended these services en masse in their traditional uniforms. It was the custom for the civic head to take the collection and for the head boy to read the lesson. Until 1787 it was the practice of the boys to go begging round the streets of York after the annual service. In that year they were given sixpence apiece by the School in order to discourage the practice.

The committee of the Schools gave a donation of £25 to the Minister of St Michael-le-Belfrey in 1785 towards re-building spacious and convenient lofts to enable the boys and girls from the two Schools to attend Divine service on Sunday afternoons, and on the occasion of the Annual Service on Good Fridays.

Printed lists of benefactors, which singled out clergymen and councillors of the City, were circulated every year. The name of Francis Drake, the historian and school surgeon, appeared in the 1745 list together with that of Thomas Gent, the well-known York printer. A descendant of the latter was admitted to the School as a pupil in 1833.

The school took in about ten to fifteen boys a year, in some cases after several unsuccessful applications for admittance, and it was quite common for two or more brothers to be at the school together. The numbers of boys in residence fluctuated between about 50 and 70 from the 1750s until the 1920s, with a temporary increase to 84 in 1872. Some 2048 boys had already passed through the school by 1888, a total which was to approach 3000 before the School finally closed its doors in 1947.

Living conditions in the School were spartan particularly with regard to heating and ventilation, warm clothing, diet and washing facilities. The domestic facilities were improved in 1780 with the installation of a privy and the sinking of a well to improve the quality and quantity of the water supply for the School. The school yard was paved in the following year. In another measure to improve living conditions Elizabeth Barber was paid £1 a year for killing rats on the premises.

Some deaths occurred amongst the pupils and the cost of a funeral at the School in 1714 was 14s.7d. of which 3s. 6d. was for the coffin, 3s. for ale and 2s. for bread rolls. The mother of the boy concerned received one shilling.

The activities and facilities of the school continued largely unchanged for the first hundred years of its existence but the school passed through a difficult period in the 1820s. The Master complained in 1821, to a sub committee appointed to manage the School, that weakly and ailing boys represented about one tenth of the School and required a disproportionate amount of the time of the staff. The Master also pointed out that it would be difficult to place these boys as apprentices.

Discipline was poor despite misdemeanours being punished by whipping the offender with a strap whilst he was carried on the back of an older boy. Absconders were required to 'run the gauntlet'. The Master was authorised in 1825 to have control and management of the boys and to use such correction as he should deem expedient. In another measure to stabilise the situation, parental visits were restricted to once a month because of the unsettling effect on the boys.

Several improvements were made in the boys' conditions in 1825 with the arrival of a new headmaster. Leather breeches were replaced by fustian trousers and warmer coats were provided. Meat and fruit pies were introduced in the diet, white bread was substituted for brown bread and Friday fast days were replaced by Friday feast days. Boiled beef and potatoes were served on Sundays and 'lashings of puddings' became the order of the day. A team of eight boys fetched and carried from the kitchen to the schoolroom, made bread, took food to the bake house and set tables. Spinning, bobbin winding and weaving activities were all discontinued and the looms removed. The traditional bedding was discarded, extra bed sheets were provided, the boys were furnished with night caps and the School was lit by gas. Coverlets were purchased for beds, together with bolsters filled with flock and pillows stuffed with feathers. Some household duties were undertaken by two or three girls from the Grey Coat School in order to provide more time for the formal education of the boys.

Despite the extensive improvements described above the Headmaster reported in March 1827 that 'great insubordination' prevailed on a recent Sunday morning when the boys locked some doors which he was compelled to break through in order to gain admission to the schoolroom. Twenty one boys were expelled for misconduct in the following year and the local reputation of the school was not very high. In 1829 a severe outbreak of bullying and beating of the smaller boys occurred with the ring leader apparently holding the school in subjection. Christmas shillings were stolen from the youngsters who were also required to hand over part of their meals or were sent over the School wall to pilfer and steal. To make matters worse the boys sang indecent songs when a mistress was unwisely put in charge of them. The School was alleged to be an asylum for the children of prostitutes and otherwise dissolute and abandoned parents. The ringleader was expelled and the standing Rules revised.

The master was absolved from blame for this state of affairs and the disciplinary problems were ascribed to the 'want of caution in the admission of children'. These problems had arisen because, from 1757 onwards, annual subscribers of 10/- or donors of £10, some 400 people in all, were entitled to participate in the admission procedures which were conducted at general meetings without any prior scrutiny of candidates.

In order to rectify this situation all applicants for admission after 1829 were screened by an annually appointed committee (the Annual Committee) of 21 members which was charged with the management, education, clothing, maintenance, apprenticeship and expulsion of pupils under the supervision of a quarterly meeting of all directors. The Annual Committee included 3 Aldermen and 3 Clergymen of the City with the senior alderman as ex officio chairman. This was a period of strong civic support from all the aldermen, ex-sheriffs and common councillors.

The opportunity was taken in 1829 to codify and extend the 81 rules governing the School. Birth certificates of candidates for admission were required to be produced before applicants were listed and preference was given to the healthiest and strongest children. After screening by the Annual Committee the eligible candidates were examined at a quarterly meeting of all subscribers before votes were cast and the names of successful candidates finally approved for admission to the Schools. Satisfactory evidence was required of the marriage of the parents, a stipulation which could only be waived if two thirds of the members present at the examination of candidates were agreeable.

The disciplinary problems did not disappear quickly and in the following year 20 out of the 64 boys in the School were expelled simultaneously and a further 11 boys were expelled in 1832 for misconduct.

The administration of the school was strengthened by a system of Visiting Directors, together with the introduction of Audit and Estate Committees. George Hudson, the so-called 'Railway King' was a member of the Estates Committee and Samuel Tuke, the Quaker businessman and social reformer, was a member of the executive committee. Joseph Rowntree was elected to the Annual Committee in 1846. Robert Davies, later a Town Clerk and local historian, successfully canvassed for the posts of treasurer, steward of the estates and secretary in 1819. He won by the narrow margin of seven votes and held the position for 10 years. He continued his interest in the Schools for nearly fifty years until his death.

The rules provided for five subscribers, not members of the Annual Committee, to serve for three years on the Estates Committee. They were required to superintend and direct the management of the estates but were not authorised to grant leases without the approval of a general meeting of subscribers. It soon became necessary to reduce rents on changes of tenancy because of the poor state of the agricultural industry.

Under another change in rules it was decided that all legacies and donations over £20 should be placed out in Government stock rather than being included in the current income of the Schools.

A further attempt to improve living conditions was made in 1829 when extensive alterations were made to the Hall at a cost of £1068. A large garden was added to the playground and £300 was spent on the purchase of land in Peaseholme Green, together with warehouses and stables, to provide rental income.

Another important innovation took place in 1829 when it was decreed that the children should undergo an annual examination in public of their scholastic ability. In addition there was to be a half yearly examination by the Annual Committee. Success in these half yearly examination was rewarded with prizes.

The revenue from lands and property was £1,100 in 1819, an amount insufficient, despite other income, to offset operating expenses. The running costs of the establishment were progressively reduced in the troublesome third decade of the century, a line of approach which may have contributed to the disciplinary problems of the School. The cost of feeding and clothing each boy fell from almost £13 per annum in 1821 to £9 in 1830.

According to the Annual Accounts for 1835 tidiness took precedence over tunefulness as the barber and the singing master were paid £1.15s. and £1.10s.6d. respectively for their services during the year.

The children of the Blue Coat and Grey Coat Schools attended services at St Michael-le-Belfrey in July 1821 and in September 1831 to celebrate the coronations of George IV and William IV respectively and were served tea and cakes after which they processed through the principal streets of the City.

Sea apprenticeships continued with two boys apprenticed to a mariner in South Shields, and one each to masters in Preston and in Skeldergate, York. The masters were required to pay the boys a total of £45 by annual instalments over 7 years with a further two guineas at the completion of the apprenticeship. The lads were to learn navigation during the time the ships were laid up and were required to provide their own sea bedding and wearing apparel.

Life at the School around this time was described by a former pupil identified only as A.O.S., in a book carrying a strong temperance message, which was published many years later in 1876. The account given by this author is in accord with other published details of life at the School in the 1820s.

Although the stated period of residence in the School extended from 9 to 14 years of age an analysis in 1838 of 64 recent leavers showed that the boys spent an average of three years and four months in the School. The majority of the boys had received no education before admittance, and parents viewed the School firstly as an institution for maintenance rather than education, and secondly, as a relief for their families rather than a benefit for the boys.

The old regime was ostensibly left behind with the appointment of William Etches and his wife who were master and mistress of the School from 1840 to 1863. With the benefit of hindsight, however, his period of office can be seen as a minor advancement rather than a radical era of improvement in the lot of the boys.

The numbers of children in the School had edged upwards, and, after the receipt in 1850 of a legacy of £2,000 from Dr Stephen Beckwith, a member of a distinguished old York family, the complement of the school was increased to 70 pupils.

CHAPTER II
The Blue Coat School 1863-1927
A progressive headmaster arrives

THE AFFAIRS OF THE SCHOOL took a marked turn for the better in December 1863 with the replacement of William Etches by Edward Robinson whose contribution to the school was probably unsurpassed by any of his predecessors or successors. Robinson was a York man, born in Fossgate, and educated at Wilson's Green Coat Boys' Charity School at Foss Bridge End which closed in 1895. He introduced a broad spectrum of changes and was credited with raising the tone of the school and the character of the scholars. The new regime was marked by an increase in the proportion of time devoted to education, a reduction in regimentation and a kindlier treatment of the pupils whose interest and support were secured by the new Headmaster and his wife.

Robinson's personal living conditions improved when he was allowed to furnish his private apartments in his own way and to increase the allowances of butter, sugar, tea and fresh milk served at the separate staff table for the Headmaster, Matron and assistant Matron. The Headmaster was allowed £1 per quarter for malt liquor, and he and the Matron were served loaf sugar which could not be adulterated so readily as loose sugar.

The boys were provided with washbasins fitted with taps and waste water pipes. One chamber utensil was provided for each of the boys' beds and the arrangement of two boys to each bed was discontinued in 1870.

Robinson encouraged promising scholars to become pupil teachers and subsequently to progress as full members of the

*Edward Robinson,
Headmaster 1863-1892.*

teaching profession. By 1871 two old scholars had become assistant teachers after obtaining Queen's scholarships and entering York Training College for schoolmasters. Four years later another old scholar was described as filling a schoolmaster appointment in Hull. The ordained headmaster of Thetford Grammar School was a former Blue Coat boy and Professor George Stephenson, who left the School in 1876, progressed from pupil teacher to a professorship at Leeds University followed by a high academic post at the University of Dublin.

Robinson also initiated a programme to train three or four pupil teachers a year to meet the needs of the Blue Coat school itself. The boys were taken on as apprentice teachers for a period of five years and were maintained and clothed by the School, They were allowed sixpence a week pocket money for the first three years, and then one shilling per week. Robinson was paid £3 annually for each pupil teacher in recognition of the extra tuition given to them. In 1889 one of the boys employed as a pupil teacher in the School was promoted to technical teacher at a salary of £20 per annum.

As a second major innovation Robinson introduced an extensive programme of evening classes on the premises for boys who had already left the School and many benefited from this opportunity to continue their education.

Marked improvements appeared in the diet and clothing of the boys including the substitution of new milk for old. Bread making at the School was revived, after it was confirmed that the procedures and quality were satisfactory. It was claimed that the boys liked this bakery work.

The teaching of French and Drawing was introduced with marked success in the School. One consequence of the focus on draughtsmanship was an increased demand for boys from the School by local employers in the mechanical trades with twelve of the leavers in 1871 going into skilled trades. In the following year it was reported that of the 17 boys who had recently left only one had become an errand boy. A room next to the bathroom was set aside for chemical experiments. Possibly as a consequence the boys fared well in the examinations of the Department of Science and Art at South Kensington.

Robinson was encouraged in these and other measures by John Ford, an influential and helpful Governor of the Blue Coat School for 14 years until his death in 1875. Ford was a notable Headmaster of Bootham School for 37 years who, by his influence, had mitigated the severity of the regime of a previous Blue Coat headmaster, a man who was described as somewhat lacking in sympathy with his orphan charges. A plaque was erected in the School to record the efforts of Ford and a fellow supporter of the School, David Hill, in improving the dormitory accommodation. Another of Robinson's supporters, Dr Shann, died in 1882 after 30 years on the Executive Committee including 12 years as chairman. A later chairman for 12 years, Jno. Francis Taylor of Holly Bank House, gave £1,000 to the Schools in 1892. The Steward and Secretary of the Charity, Edward Peters died in 1898 after holding the appointments for nearly 50 years and was succeeded by his son J.A.Peters, a local solicitor. These various supporters provided a remarkable degree of continuity in the affairs of the School in the second and third quarters of the nineteenth century.

The new headmaster was instrumental in founding an Old Scholars Association in 1865 partly as a means of assessing, at annual reunions, how far the School had been instrumental in advancing the advancement and welfare of Old Boys in the outside world. 90 old scholars attended a reunion on Boxing Day 1866, the customary day for such events. After an address of welcome on these occasions a paper was usually presented by one of the company. The popularity of these events was illustrated by the numbers of attenders which had increased to 120 within six years. The Association supported a Library Fund, also established by Robinson, to furnish the pupils with suitable recreational literature.

Further innovations by Robinson included the establishment of a Friendly Society in 1872 and a School Benevolent Society in 1877. The latter provided supplementary assistance, under strictly specified circumstances, to needy apprentices who had attended the school. The Friendly Society provided sickness and death benefits for former pupils and their dependants. It met on the school site and thus avoided the tendency towards an excessive consumption of alcohol sometimes associated with Friendly Societies which met on licensed premises. Members were admitted to the organisation from 14 to 40 years of age with the rates of subscriptions linked to the age of admission. The Society had a favourable claims experience, attributed to prudent management combined with a restricted membership, and refunded 10% of contributions to subscribers annually. The scheme was wound up in 1912 and its remaining funds of £47 were given to the School

The Schools continued to extend their land holdings and in 1866 acquired for £1,450 the outstanding 50% of their shared holding at Knapton which had originally been purchased by Queen Anne's bounty to augment the living at Kirby Wharfe. Rent rebates of £5 or £10 a quarter were allowed to agricultural tenants of the Charity during the farming depression in the fourth quarter of the century.

In the 1880s the boys were invited annually to the 'Hollies' at Dringhouses, the home of Aldermen John Close, where they played cricket, ate a sumptuous tea and were given several shillings apiece for their savings accounts with the advice 'a nimble ninepence makes a sure shilling'. The alderman, who was Lord Mayor in 1892, also gave the boys a florin (two shillings) apiece after the public examinations. Other leisure activities included day outings to Scarborough, Naburn Lock and a farm at Flaxton. In another of his many constructive acts of generosity to the Schools, Mr Close offered £50 towards the costs of teaching the rudiments of joinery work, cobbling and tailoring to the boys in their spare time. Lathes and tools were provided and the workshops, on the upper floor of a warehouse in Peaseholme Green, were supervised by the appropriate tradesmen. The emphasis was now on industrial skills rather than simple shoe-mending and clothes repairing. Boys who had shown diligence and skill in the workshops were presented with £2 and Gladstone bags by Alderman Close. In the longer term this initiative by the alderman ensured that Blue Coat boys could perform as domestic handymen in later life. In the shorter term these acquired skills enhanced the job prospects of boys aspiring to trade apprenticeships.

The boys participated in the celebrations connected with the Golden Jubilee of Queen Victoria and each received a medal with a photograph of the Queen on one side and the Arms of York on the reverse. They attended a grand Military Review on the Knavesmire and joined 13,000 Sunday school pupils at an entertainment in Bootham Park provided by the Lord Mayor and Corporation. Similar celebrations took place ten years later for the Diamond Jubilee.

The school continued to steer the leavers into secure trades, rather than let them drift into short-term paid work as errand boys. This was achieved partly by subsidising their board and lodging, where necessary, with the assistance of the Benevolent Society. During this period of the nineteenth century some leavers were taught husbandry and others were put to service with so-called respectable families. Of the 75 boys who left the school between 1875 and 1883 39 found work as artisans, 11 as clerks and 7 in retail establishments. The high death rate of boys and young men was brought out in a more extensive analysis of the 425 boys admitted to the school in the preceding quarter century. Five boys had died in school and 27 had died since leaving school. Of the remainder, 163 became mechanics or skilled workmen, 54 had become clerks, 25 had joined the Colours as soldiers or sailors, 13 were school teachers and 9 had emigrated. The importance of the railway industry as an employer of labour was reflected in the 45 old scholars employed by the North Eastern Company. The rapid expansion of the local confectionery industry at the end of the nineteenth century is illustrated by the employment of three leavers by Rowntree and Company in 1893, two in the following year and a further four in 1897.

Some boys were unable to find apprenticeships or other jobs despite the efforts of the headmaster, old scholars and subscribers. These boys, in accordance with rigidly applied rules, were sent out of the school at 14 years of age either to their parents or in to the charge of the appropriate parish officers.

The changes introduced by Robinson generated a temporary improvement in subscription income which advanced from £338 in 1868 to £570 in 1882 and then fell away again to £361 over the next twenty years. This decline reflected a significant reduction in financial support from the Anglican clergy coupled with a smaller reduction in contributions from the civic representatives. It was argued at the time that this lack of a lead from the clergy and Corporation contributed to a falling off in support from the general public. It was recommended that the annual Anniversary Service be revived as a means of engendering civic and financial support for the school.

The School premises at St Anthony's Hall had been leased by the Corporation from the outset in return for a modest rental. A 75 year extension of this lease was negotiated in 1868 before building extensions were put in hand.

A classroom was added to the school in 1871, followed by the provision - over an extended period of twenty five years - of a new laundry, improved heating and new hand basins. The earth closets were replaced by water closets in 1897 at a cost of £175 'on the automatic system of Adams & Co.,' the near neighbours of the School on Peaseholme Green. A wet weather play shed measuring sixty feet by twenty feet was erected soon afterwards. The gallery, a long-standing feature of the school room was removed in the final year of the century.

The School reached its peak number of 84 boys in 1872, a year in which the two Charity Schools ran at a combined deficit of £550. In view of the scale of this deficit it was considered inexpedient to increase further the numbers of pupils in either the boys' or the girls' schools.

The Treasurer of the Schools, Robert Swann, was requested to resign in 1879 when the local bank of which he was a partner, Messrs Swann Clough, failed. The Headmaster was idemnified by the Committee against losses on Notes of the bank and the Executive Committee commenced legal action for balances owing to the Schools in their accounts with the bank.

Edward Robinson died in 1892 after 28 years as Headmaster during which time he was credited with having trained orphan boys to be self-reliant, useful and happy men. He was described as having filled his post with zeal and efficiency and his portrait was placed in the dining room of the School. Robinson was succeeded by H.L.Hunter, an Old Boy of the School, who carried on the improvements initiated by Robinson and introduced systematic swimming training in 1893.

The bi-centenary of the two Schools was celebrated in 1905 with a service in the Minster and a re-union attended by 180 old pupils and their spouses. The assembled company sat down to tea in the Exhibition Buildings and stayed on for an entertainment of songs, recitations and musical drill. Commemorative plaques were presented to the two Schools. The occasion was marked by the publication of a souvenir booklet edited by Moses B. Cotsworth, an Old Boy, which included a spirited appeal for funds for the School. Cotsworth took the opportunity in the book of advocating the renewal of the custom of the Lord Mayor entertaining the children at the Mansion House after the annual service as a means of maintaining interest in the Schools at trifling cost. Cotsworth also regretted the decline in the support for the school by the clergy and Council members.

It was recorded in the bi-centenary booklet that in the past 200 years the Charity had received legacies amounting to £68,294.

The Rules of the Schools were revised in 1904 when the membership of the Annual Committee was increased from 21 to 25, its

Old Blue Coat Scholars 1905 (some with their wives).

name changed to the Permanent Committee, and the quorum specified as nine members. Confusingly this group was also known as the Executive Committee, or - in its dealings with the Grey Coat School - simply as the 'Gentlemen'. The rules for electing children to places in the Schools remained largely unchanged. No child could be admitted to the Schools without the recommendation of two directors and the names of all candidates were scrutinised by either the Permanent Committee or, in the case of girls, the Ladies Committee before being circulated to every director for votes to be cast. Canvassing of votes for boys seeking admission to the School was frowned upon after printed cards requesting support for a candidate appeared in 1873.

The all-male Permanent Committee met monthly to manage and direct the Boys' School and superintend the Girls' School. Its role in the Boys' School was to regulate the education, clothing and maintenance of the boys and deal with expulsions from the School. In later years the monthly meetings of the Permanent Committee were delegated to a smaller house committee. A sub-committee of five ladies assisted the Permanent Committee with the domestic arrangements of the Boys' School. The Secretary of the School, acting on behalf of the Permanent Committee, was punctilious in

Old Grey Coat Scholars 1905 (some with their husbands).

acknowledging gifts and other services rendered to the Schools in minutes, annual reports, the local Press and by personal letters of thanks, and these kindnesses were included in the Annual report for all to see. In accordance with a long standing tradition boys were presented to the members of the Permanent Committee when they left the School.

An education sub-committee met quarterly and a finance sub-committee met as necessary. The Real Estate Committee now comprised twelve trustees selected from the Directors.

The numbers of candidates put forward for admission fell off in the early 1900s when the Permanent Committee claimed that it was experiencing difficulty in making the facilities offered by the Schools known in the City. Newspaper advertisements were used to encourage candidates to come forward. A subsequent shortage of children for admission in 1910 was followed by a call to clergymen of all denominations, schoolmasters and members of the medical profession to nominate suitable candidates. These shortages of candidates probably reflected an improvement in local economic conditions coupled with enhanced local education facilities.

The decline in subscriptions continued to be a matter of concern for the Gentlemen. This situation was aggravated in 1909 when it was considered necessary to spend money on bringing the farm buildings on the various land holdings up to standard.

H.L.Hunter died in 1911 after nearly twenty years in charge and was succeeded by Mr and Mrs H.C. Hughes as Headmaster and Matron. During his time in office Hunter consolidated the reforms introduced by his more high profile predecessor and encouraged the musical activities of the School including a concert given by the boys in the Assembly Rooms. It was claimed during Hunter's period as Headmaster that the School inculcated self reliance and independence and that the boys were trained to accept responsibility and know how to use it.

Mr Hughes was assigned a wider range of tasks than his predecessor. It was his responsibility in the future to obtain suitable situations for the boys.

Changes in social habits emerged when problems were encountered in arranging the timing of the Annual Service. Good Friday was no longer a suitable day for the service because many Councillors treated Easter as a holiday week-end which they spent away from York.

In a new venture the boys were taken to a summer camp at Scarborough and homeless boys were placed in suitable farmhouses in the country for the remainder of the school holidays.

The facilities of the School were modernised gradually, including the introduction of additional bathroom accommodation in 1911. In order to conform with Education Department requirements an isolation unit and a gymnasium, together with three bright airy new classrooms, were built in 1914 at a cost of £1200. This development was described as the most extensive and significant in the history of the School. By way of celebration at the opening ceremony the boys and girls were 'regaled with added fare to that usually provided'. Part of the cost was defrayed by a special appeal, which despite being scaled down because of the outbreak of war in August 1914, raised £718. The gymnasium was developed by strengthening the floor of the Hall which ceased to be used as classrooms. Boxing gloves were available in the gymnasium for those who had quarrels to settle.

The Annual Reunion of Old Boys and the Annual Camp were cancelled after the outbreak of war in August 1914. Thereafter the boys were boarded out in the country during the summer holidays. The Anniversary Service was held as usual with the Archbishop of York preaching the sermon. Three years later the Service was postponed because of an outbreak of measles.

Two Belgian boy refugees were maintained at the School in late 1914 with the cost defrayed by the staff and boys. The Belgians were replaced in the following year by two French refugees whose father had originally hailed from York.

The staff of the school in 1915 consisted of the head master and three assistant teachers together with a tailor, cobbler and general maintenance man. The headmaster's wife held the post of matron and supervised a cook, housemaid and serving maid. There were many changes of teaching staff during the war years as fit men departed and were replaced with those in lower medical categories, including a male teacher from the Blue Coat School in Oldham. Fortunately for the School the Headmaster was exempted from military service after an appeal to an adjudicating Tribunal. The first woman teacher, Miss Olive Rhodes, was appointed in 1916. Despite the educational disruption caused by changes of staff during the war years two boys secured places at Archbishop Holgate's School by 1917 and a third boy joined them in 1919. These boys were allowed to continue living at the Hall.

Food was rationed and, although the School was able to keep within its allowances for meat and sugar, problems were experienced with flour supplies.

Schools were required to fit black-out blinds on windows. On May 2nd 1916 the premises suffered slight damage, but no casualties, during an air raid by a Zeppelin airship on York when a bomb fell in Aldwark opposite the Hall. The School was illuminated by gas at the time of the raid - a lighting system which was replaced by electricity some two years later.

An Old Boy, J.R. Paxton who was at the School from 1915, gave an account of life in the institution at the time of the first World War. Paxton won a scholarship to Archbishop Holgate's School before becoming a a pupil teacher for two years. He left the Blue

Coat School at 18 years of age for teacher training at St John's College in York. In later years he became Headmaster of a village school in the Cotswolds.

In his comprehensive account he describes how entrants were provided with a set of clothes including a nightshirt. The new day began at 5.45 a.m. with a roll-call by the head monitor. Bedding was folded into a prescribed pattern with the stripes on the blankets neatly aligned. This was followed by floor sweeping and dusting to make the class rooms ready for use. The boys then undertook their specialist tasks which had been brought to a high pitch of order and efficiency by frequent repetition and youthful ingenuity.

Prayers and hymns were followed by breakfast in the dining room where one table was reserved for the unfortunate bed-wetters who at one time slept in a separate dormitory known as 'Paradise'. Breakfast consisted of two slices of bread and margarine with a mug of cocoa. The bread ration was reduced to a slice and a half in winter when porridge was served. There was playtime before and after lessons which occupied five and a half hours of the day. Six boys peeled eight large buckets of potatoes during the mid-day break. Each evening a coal-coke-stick team chopped kindling into 15 sticks for a boiler, 12 sticks for the bakehouse oven and 7 sticks for a small fire. The stick-shed and alley-boys riddled ashes and clinker in the alley between the school wall and the churchyard wall of St Cuthbert's Church. After tea at 5.45 p.m. the younger boys played card and board games and the older boys made fretwork articles from plywood. The library was quite well stocked and comics could be traded at a shop with buying and selling prices of a halfpenny and a farthing respectively.

On Saturdays a different set of routines came into play. Five boys were assigned to the laundry where two of the team used six-legged peggles in the peggy tubs, one boy scrubbed collars and cuffs, and another member washed towels. Fifteen boys were employed in teams scrubbing and cleaning in the dining room, cleaning the hall and stone steps, and sweeping indoors and outdoors. One boy cleaned the windows on Wednesdays with another boy assigned the important job of holding the ladder. One boy pumped the organ and another kept up the supply of steam from the boiler.

Wednesday evenings were taken up with sock darning and prizes were given annually for the best darners. The boys were responsible for three pairs of socks apiece which were discarded when it took more than four ounces of wool to darn them. Three boys were employed in the bakehouse where the baking of a batch of 28 loaves, weighing 7lbs. apiece, took place on Tuesday and Friday afternoons. The boys slipped out of classes in the mornings to check that the preparatory stages of the bread-making process were proceeding satisfactorily. The bakers enjoyed the privileges of creeping in beside the ovens to keep warm on winter days and of supplementing their diet with unofficial hot bread cakes. Saturday afternoons were reserved for games on Monk Stray or swimming at St George's baths. Concert parties, which had been formed during the war years to entertain the troops, provided entertainments on Saturday evenings in the post-war years.

On Sunday mornings the boys were marched in a 'crocodile', and in traditional uniform, to St Saviour's Church in Saviourgate. On Sunday afternoons the lads attended church at St Michael-le-Belfrey. No outdoor games were allowed on Sundays. Instead a master sometimes read a story to the assembled company.

Personal cleanliness was achieved by a bath ritual in which the younger boys were soaped in a bath, shaped like an armchair, under the supervision of older boys. After a preliminary rinsing the boys were inspected by the master on duty before a final rinse was taken in a plunge bath filled with warm water. At this time a barber visited the School once a month to cut the boy's hair, a doubtful privilege not enjoyed by the girls whose hair was 'styled' in-house.

Outgoing mail was vetted by a master. Visiting relatives and friends were allowed into the school for half an hour between 2 p.m. and 6 p.m. on the first Friday in the month. Special visiting and other arrangements were made for boys who, as a result of war time admission changes, hailed from as far afield as Middlesborough, Doncaster and Sheffield.

The school tailor, an ex-county cricketer, had his own workroom in the School. Clothing was made in graduated sizes from 1 to 70 and each boy was allotted a number, which corresponded with the number on his locker, during a sizing operation at the beginning of the school year. These numbers were printed on every item of clothing. When boots and shoes were sent for repair replacements were fished out of the communal boot cupboard. The boys were provided with three sets of corduroy trousers and two coats for winter wear. Summer wear consisted of tweed trousers and blue drill striped blazers. Blue trousers were worn on Sundays with smooth Melton cloth coats in winter and swallow tail coats with gold braid and gilt buttons in summer. Narrow blue and white check bow ties were worn in school and broader white linen bow ties were worn on Sundays in the winter. Blue striped shirts were changed once a week and boys in the choir wore celluloid collars with a bow tie. On Sundays in the summer a bib was worn, tied at the back of the neck. For ordinary wear the head gear comprised a blue cap with yellow stripes from the crown down to the brim. Best head gear consisted of a pork-pie sailor-type hat complete with a rim and surrounded by gold braid.

Life at the school was spartan, the fare was meagre and bullying by older boys and prefects was rife. Up to one third of the boys ran away at some time during their stay at the school. Food supplies provided by relatives were plundered, or depleted by various forms of extortion.

As consolation for the loss of some treats under war-time conditions the auditors of the Charity, Messrs Pulleyn, Creer & Co., offered to pay for a monthly visit to the Picture House for the pupils. The secretaries of the two schools were required to vet the suitability of the entertainment on offer.

Entry to the school continued to be conducted by ballot with 850 voting papers circulated each quarter. The name of one boy was withdrawn by his friends after four unsuccessful appearances on the ballot papers. Maintenance payments for children by parents or outside bodies were the exception at this stage and a parent from Doncaster, who was willing to pay £20 per annum maintenance for his son in 1916, was informed that the Rules of the School did not provide for fee-paying entrants.

A sizeable sale of land holdings took place in 1901 when 17 acres of plantation at Loftus Green was sold for £2,000. By 1917 the country was experiencing a shortage of timber for war and civilian purposes so the Estates Committee decided to fell all the available timber on its land holdings.

The opportunity was taken in November 1917 to value the Estate controlled by the Charity Schools. It was estimated that the 470 acres of agricultural property had a sale value of £15,300, some £4,300 less than the book value. Two years later the total rents from these properties amounted to £583, less £33 tithes.

The Permanent Committee decided in 1919 to withdraw from land investment after 150 years of such ventures. Later the same year the Estates Committee wrote to all tenants, including the tenant at Knapton who was an Old Blue Coat boy, seeking offers for the property they occupied. The sums eventually realised for the majority of the properties, amounting to £15,175, were around the previously calculated book values. The number of Trustees of the property of the Charity Schools, which had fallen over the years from seventeen to two, was restored to twenty with Henry Rhodes Brown as Chairman.

Rhodes Brown had entered the School as a pupil in 1873, was elected to the Annual Committee in 1907 and appointed Chairman of the Permanent Committee in 1917. Mrs Rhodes Brown was elected to the Ladies Committee in 1906.

It was decided that legacies of up to £250, and subsequently £500, could be used for the running expenses of the School, a significant increase on the figure of £100 which had been in force since 1912. It was also agreed to transfer £5,295 to the ordinary account to liquidate a deficit which arisen from increased operating costs during the war years.

During the final year of the War it was suggested that the School should cease to be an educational institution and that the children should be transferred to local elementary schools. Successful counter-arguments were put forward to maintain the status quo. For example it was claimed that the pupils would bring infections back into the School from the outside world, and that the boys would not be able to carry out their domestic duties before and between school hours, with the consequent necessity to employ paid labour.

A small reduction in running costs of about £40 per annum was achieved in 1918 when York Corporation agreed, for the first time, to waive payment of rent in recognition of the public work which the School was carrying out in maintaining and educating needy children. The Corporation replaced an annual payment for property maintenance of £40 by a token yearly rent of one shilling and agreed to remain responsible for those parts of the property belonging to them.

The Old Boys Association paid for the repair and restoration of the school organ as a War Memorial to servicemen educated at the School. The organ had been installed in 1858 and cleaned in 1897. It was finally removed in 1932.

The financial affairs of the School improved in 1919 when it was classified as an Institution School under Section 15 of the 1902 Education Act. In order to qualify for the accompanying State, as opposed to Local Authority, grant of thirty six shillings per head the pupils were required to attend for 400 out of the 415 half days for which the School was open in the year. The School was now required to provide Religious Instruction in conformity with the directions of the Church of England. Two years later the School was placed on a list of approved Institutions by the Board of Education. The Permanent Committee decided that it was no longer appropriate to use the designation 'Charity Schools' which was removed from all documentation except where it was legally necessary.

The treasurer of the Schools, Mr J.R.Hill died in 1919. He and his father had been members of the Executive Committee for nearly 50 years and, apart from being generous donors, both had devoted much time to the affairs of the Blue Coat School. Mr and Mrs Hill and their daughter had also been prominent in supporting the Grey Coat School.

The composition of the Permanent Committee changed significantly in 1920 when two Ladies were co-opted for the first time together with one representative each from two major local firms, Messrs Rowntrees and Messrs Leetham. A major alteration in the financing of the Schools occurred in the same year when it was agreed that a limited number of children would be admitted whose parents or guardians were prepared to pay maintenance costs. The names of these children did not appear on the voting lists as candidates for admission but the scale of contribution, or pension in the case of children of deceased Servicemen, was indicated on the lists of children accepted for entry.

A third important change occurred in 1920 with the departure of the Headmaster, H.C. Hughes, to the larger Blue Coat Institution in Liverpool. He had lost his only son in action during the War and his wife died soon afterwards. Eighty three candidates put themselves forward for his job and, in an expansion of his role, the incoming headmaster was allocated responsibility for collecting subscriptions on a commission basis.

The School still possessed a strong institutional flavour aggravated by the arrival and departure of two unsatisfactory headmasters, one of whom was asked to resign after an unsatisfactory report from H.M. Inspectors in 1927. This report criticised the absence of a scheme of work for the school and poor time-keeping. It was noted that the school required a firm hand to improve discipline and the premises needed to be cleaned properly. The school registers were lost in transit to London and the Honorary Secretary was unable to get papers, receipts and books from the outgoing Headmaster. In an attempt to offset the poor image of the school, concerts and lectures were introduced together with a prize-winning Sword Dancing group. Sporting activities were expanded to include a Rugby League team. Dress standards were relaxed and the boys were allowed to wear shorts in school, and in the playground, except on Sundays and other special occasions. A further proposal to improve the image and facilities of the School, by moving out to the suburbs, was abandoned in 1923 as impracticable.

There was no procession to the Church for the Anniversary Service in 1924 and the service was postponed for two months in 1926 because of the General Strike.

Details of five minor charities assisting the School were published in the minutes for 1924. These were Huttons's charity belonging to the parish of St Crux which donated £20 annually, York Charitable Society which donated £38 annually, Ellis charity which made an annual educational grant of £20 on request,

Wilson's gift of £1 annually from land at Easingwold and Hanson's charity which provided £2 per annum from land at Langwith. Other income came from collecting boxes placed in Working Men's clubs. Fund raising continued to be a major concern for the Permanent Committee and house to house collections were instituted with collectors paid a 10% commission. York Corporation distributed the proceeds of military tattoos on the Knavesmire to charitable and other causes and the Schools received £2000 from this source in 1926.

The Bluecoat School undertook to provide teaching accommodation for girls from the Greycoat School in 1923 and the educational facilities were improved with the opening of new science laboratories in 1931. A surgery replaced the kitchen table as the medical treatment centre in 1928. In the same year a new concrete playground was laid down and the backlog of war-time property maintenance was finally completed.

Operating economies were sought in 1924 to offset mounting deficits and it was decided to forego elections to vacant places in the School. Every quarterly election cost between £8 and £10 for printing and postage.

CHAPTER III
The Blue Coat School 1927-1947 Heyday and closure

MR CECIL T.B. AMOS WAS appointed Headmaster in 1927 and the years preceding the Second World War under his headmastership constituted a high point for the school and its pupils. Several boys gained scholarships to local secondary or grammar schools and some progressed to Universities. Amos, not always a fit man, worked hard to improve the standards of the school and it was reported in 1934 that 'the tone of the school, the personal appearance and general condition of the scholars, as well as their attitude to work, are particularly fine'. Mr Amos held a joint appointment with Mrs Amos, as Matron, playing a full part in bringing about the results achieved by the School.

The impact made by Amos helped to maintain for the time being the support of subscribers to the schools who numbered 349 in 1929. Of these 190 paid the minimum sum of ten shillings necessary to qualify for a vote for candidates for admission to the two schools. Unfortunately the numbers of subscribers gradually declined in the 1930s and the subscription income declined by nearly 20% in 1936 alone, a situation which was safeguarded to some extent by a capital fund amounting to £61,287. Failure to collect agreed maintenance payments from parents contributed to an operating deficit of £1,007 in the year, a sum equivalent to the cost of maintaining 10 children in the Schools. The average annual deficit for the 10 years to 1935 was £459. In an attempt to offset this outflow of resources Alderman Rhodes Brown raised £834 by a special appeal for funds in 1933 when he was Lord Mayor.

*Cecil T.B. Amos,
Headmaster 1927-1946.*

Amos had an interest in the stage and directed his first production at the age of eleven in his home town of Nuneaton. He produced annual pantomimes at the School in order to raise funds for the Annual Camp on the coast. He became more ambitious with these productions over the years and tried to find a part for every boy in the school, on one occasion casting the two smallest boys as 'Buttercup' and 'Daisy' in Cinderella. The shows were usually supported by the Civic Party and the Dean of York. An excerpt from the 1935 pantomime, Robin Hood, was broadcast on the North Regional Programme of the BBC, an indication of the standard achieved by Amos. During the programme the headmaster gave a talk on the history of the School from the stage in St Anthony's Hall. Mrs Amos acted as Wardrobe Mistress and the Theatre Royal loaned wigs and costumes. The preparation of scenery and props extended the skills of the boys.

There was a link with reality in the 1938 pantomime, 'Dick Whittington', when the leading character invested a Blue Coat boy on stage as Sheriff. Sitting in the audience was the Sheriff of York, Councillor William Thompson, himself a Blue Coat boy.

Amos organised many other activities in a stylish manner. He provided a printed programme with train times and high tides for the summer camp at Filey in 1930 when, typically, the programme included a visit to an England v Australia cricket match at Scarborough, a tour over H.M.S. York, boat trips, a visit to a concert party show, rambles, sand castle competitions and a sports day. . A large army hut served as a dining hall and the boys slept in tents. Several friends of the school provided 'treats' such as a visit to a circus. Mr John Saville took cine films of several subsequent camps which he then titled and projected at social gatherings. An amusing sound track was added to these films in the 1980s by Chris Webb and his family. The planning of School activities was eased with the installation of a telephone at the Hall in 1932. The school and Headmaster shared the cost and Amos was charged for his private calls.

The diversified school programme in the Silver Jubilee Year of King George V and Queen Mary in 1935, amply justified the comment of the writer of the Annual Report in that year that 'socially the year has been a record one'. Over 2000 people attended the nine performances of the School Pantomime, including three performances for the unemployed and inmates of other institutions in York. The proceeds helped to finance a fortnight's holiday under canvas at Filey with transport provided by Alderman W.H. Birch. At other times the lads enjoyed swimming and woodwork and danced the 'Norfolk Long Dance' at the Yorkshire Folk Dancing competitions. Eight boys entertained the Grey Coat girls with a mouth organ concert.

In the same year, 1935, twenty of the senior boys undertook a day trip to London which packed into 25 hours almost every event and tourist attraction in the Metropolis including an early morning visit to Billingsgate fish market, attendance at a service of Holy Communion in St Pauls and a view of the King and Queen setting off on their Jubilee drive round the East End. A similar trip was arranged two years later for a party of senior boys to attend the Coronation celebrations. Other events in 1935 included the camp at Filey, a tea party to celebrate the Silver Jubilee and an end of term party at Christmas. The boys undertook route-lining as Guards of Honour, firstly on a visit by Royalty and secondly, on Mayor-making day. In a subsequent encounter with Royalty the children formed a guard of honour when the new King and Queen visited Terry's factory in 1937.

Two boys were baptised prior to confirmation in the early 1930s using a centuries-old Damascus treasure box as a font. This wooden box with a shallow lid was given by Mr Lance Foster and housed in the School Museum.

The Old Boys Association, which was revived in 1933 with over 100 members, after a lapse of nearly 10 years, ran a successful cricket team in the York Evening League. The Association produced its own magazine in which old boys took advertisements showing that some were builders, painters and decorators, boot repairers, bakers, shopfitters, plumbers, and publicans. A very full programme was mounted including annual outings, reunion dinners, dances, whist drives and dramatic performances. The Old Boys and the York Cooperative Society both provided representatives on the Annual Committee.

Canon A.R. Gill bequeathed £40 for the re-decoration of the bosses in St Anthony's Hall in 1937 including the centre boss with its representation of a pig, the symbol of St Anthony. School amenities were improved in the same year with the addition of a library and recreation room. The boys constructed a greenhouse and poultry house and received practical instruction in their use as well as keeping the school fully supplied with eggs. The school gardens were highly praised by sightseers walking along the City Walls behind the school. These ventures opened up new employment opportunities and several boys obtained jobs as poultry keepers.

The School received visitors from overseas and the travel agents, Thomas Cook, were asked to include the Schools on a list of places worth visiting in York.

Miss Elizabeth Gray resigned as honorary secretary of the School in 1930 and was succeeded by Colonel Warren, himself an Old Boy of the School, who also became treasurer in 1937. The Colonel had organised postal services in the Middle East during the First World War and then became Head Postmaster of York.

He decided to devote his retirement years to the Schools and camped with the boys at Filey in 1937 when he was Sheriff of York.

A new playing field and a sports pavilion at Stray Garth off Stockton Lane, for use by both schools, were opened by the Princess Royal during the Annual Sports Day in 1938. She was presented with a souvenir booklet by the Mooring twins who were the smallest boy and girl in the Schools. The pavilion was named in memory of Alderman Henry Rhodes Brown, an Old Boy of the School, who was twice Lord Mayor of York in 1913-14 and 1932-33 and also Chairman of the School Governors. The Old Boys financed part of the scheme as a tribute to Rhodes Brown and occupied their own pavilion on the same site. The Sheriff on that occasion was Alderman William Thompson, another Old Boy, who went on to become Lord Mayor of York in 1943-4. The playing field project cost £1,000 and a two day bazaar at the school organised by the Matron, Mrs Amos, contributed £200 towards this sum. The debt on the field was finally cleared off by a later two-day bazaar at the Assembly Rooms followed by a dance in the evening.

The boys celebrated their improved sporting facilities by winning the York Schools League Cricket Cup in 1938. T.Sanderson was awarded a bat autographed by Herbert Sutcliffe for the most outstanding performance in a series of matches. Sutcliffe, the Yorkshire and England cricketer, had attended an indoor camp fire at the School some years previously. This famous sportsman was apparently the most notable visitor to the School since Mr William Gladstone, the Victorian politician, in 1847.

Details of the subsequent careers of several Old Boys of the School emerged in 1933 with pride of place extravagantly given to Moses B. Cotsworth the author of the 1905 Bi-centenary souvenir book. Cotsworth was acclaimed as a man 'whose service in financial circles once surpassed those of the Bank of England and who is now, at the request of the League of Nations, working on the revised calendar in various countries of the world'. He was an advocate of the thirteen month year.

Amongst other successful Old Boys were Mr Cremmett who was Postmaster of Derby, George Whitwell who was governor of the largest reformatory school in England, and James Ashton who was head of Art Museums throughout Australia. In 1931 Leslie Charlton had been awarded a scholarship by the Ministry of Agriculture to the Agricultural College at Nantwich, Cheshire, a good example of the successful changes in the classrooms initiated by Amos.

In most years an Anniversary Service was held at the Minster, St Michael-le-Belfrey or St Helen's Church, attended by the Civic Party in full ceremonial robes. The occasion began with the children in traditional costume leading the Civic Party in procession from the Mansion House to the church. In accordance with tradition the collection in aid of the School was taken by the Lord Mayor and Sheriff and the Head Boy of the School read the Lesson. The Civic Party, together with the booted and spurred Chief Constable and other assembled dignitaries, then in their turn led the pupils in procession back to the Mansion House where parents and friends of both the boys and girls schools were entertained by the pupils. The latter were presented with prizes and gifts of an orange, an apple and sixpence to commemorate the occasion. These Services were notable events in the local Civic calendar, and a typical example was described by H.V. Morton in an article for a U.S. newspaper in 1928 which was subsequently reprinted in his well-known book 'In Search of England'. Morton remarked on 'The Lord Mayor and Sheriff walking in state with the sword of the Emperor Sigismund before a regiment of orphans'.

The Schools were closely linked with the Civic Party in 1933-4. The Lord Mayor, H.E. Harrowell, and Lady Mayoress were valued members of the Gentlemen's and Ladies' Committees respectively and the Sheriff, H.L. Creer was the auditor of the accounts of the Charity.

Applications exceeded vacancies for the first time for many years in 1933 when a change in Rules brought about the elimination of the ballot. Vacancies thereafter were filled on the recommendation of the re-constituted Executive Committee which consisted of the Lord Mayor, three members of the Corporation of the City and 22 members elected by the subscribers. Places on the Committee were no longer reserved for Anglican clergymen.

Entrance to the School was confined primarily to children belonging to York or its immediate neighbourhood but applications continued to be entertained on behalf of children living in other localities if the Schools were supported by subscribers living in those areas. Parents or guardians were required, as in the past, to relinquish control and management of the children and to assign authority to the School to place the children in a trade or service. Parents were allowed to visit their children provided, as in 1829, 'they come clean in person and dress and conduct themselves in an orderly manner and do not under any circumstances give the children any kind of eatables'. From the early 1920s onwards fees were paid for an increasing proportion of the scholars. The collection of these fees proved to be an onerous task for the Honorary Treasurers and the task was handed over in 1939 to a firm of professional debt collectors.

Alderman Rhodes Brown retired as Chairman of the Permanent Committee in January 1936 because of ill-health and Mr E.J. Rymer succeeded him. He in turn was followed in the Chair in 1942 by Alderman Thompson, a prominent grocer in York with shops in Goodramgate and Micklegate, who was the second Old Boy to achieve the highest Civic offices.

In the second quarter of the present century the children were encouraged to compete for York City scholarships. Three boys at Nunthorpe School, Frank Ware, George Robinson, and Harry Glover, were well placed in their class performance lists in 1935. Robinson and Glover went on to gain their Bachelor of Science degrees at Leeds University and Ware obtained a similar qualification at Sheffield University. Whilst awaiting call-up for the Royal Air Force Ware helped at the school which met the cost of his academic cap and gown.

Successful scholarship candidates were allowed to remain at St Anthony's Hall until the completion of their awards and, to enable them to prepare their school homework, were excused from the traditional highly organised teams which continued to carry out such domestic chores as baking, laundering and fire-lighting. The bakery activity ceased in 1936 in favour of local bakers. Now and then the boys enjoyed pork pies for breakfast on Sunday mornings when Whittakers, a local bakery, handed over unsold stocks on Saturday evenings. The children continued to be completely clothed on their final departure in the form of one suit of clothes, one pair of boots, one handkerchief and two shirts, vests, collars and ties

In early 1939 the Schools agreed to take two male and two female German refugee children of Protestant faith aged seven to nine years. In a subsequent wartime development several mothers with husbands serving in H.M. Forces successfully sought admission to the Schools for their children to enable the mothers to undertake various forms of war work.

The Headmaster and his wife arranged a whist drive in the autumn of 1940 and used the proceeds to send a five shilling postal order, a Christmas card and a letter from Mrs Amos to the 22 old Scholars in H.M. Forces who had kept in touch with them. Amongst their number were Petty Officer Lawrence, a submariner, who was awarded a D.S.M., and Corporal Andrews who was decorated for gallantry at Tobruk. In 1943 it was estimated that 50-60 Old Boys were serving in H.M. Forces.

Accounts of life at the School during this period suggest that bullying by the older boys and prefects continued as in former years. Small boys were subjected to electric shocks, forced to walk a plank projecting out of an upper window, or compelled to cross the communal bath by traversing a pipe. Older boys donned fearsome masks from the School Museum to frighten the younger boys after dark. Snorers in the dormitories were a particular target for heavy-handed treatment by their neighbours. One Old Boy commented that the experience of coping with these various tribulations stood him in good stead in later years when he joined H.M. Forces.

An unusual item in the minutes of the Monthly Committee in 1941 referred to a demand from the Town Clerk of York for a finely carved table of the Joiners' Guild to be handed over for use in the Committee Room of York City Council. The request was refused and the table continues to be on display in St Anthony's Hall.

Incendiary bombs fell on the Blue Coat School premises during an air raid on 29 April 1942. Some of the older boys were called from an air raid shelter to put out the fires in the stables and Mr Heppell, an Old Boy who occupied premises next to the School, was commended for his valuable services in extinguishing the flames. There was no school on the following day. The boys subsequently received training from the Fire Service in safety measures such as escaping from a smoke filled room.

The sermon at the Anniversary Service in 1944 was preached by the Rev. T. Eland, an old scholar and Vicar of Coalbrook Dale, Shropshire. The Sports Day that year was a protracted affair with 45 events including a St Christopher Race, a Bunny Run, a Plant Pot race, an Elephant Race and Mothers' Tug of War (Town v Country). At the Christmas celebrations Mr W.B. Steele delighted the boys by 'really coming down the chimney' in seasonal costume. The last joint service of the two schools was held at St Michael-le-Belfrey in 1946 when the girls wore neat dresses and blue-ribboned bonnets. The boys wore the traditional blue uniform with cravats. After the service prizes were distributed by the Lady Mayoress and gifts by the Sheriff's Lady. The gifts of money were intended to be spent on sweets which were subject to rationing for several years to come.

A shortfall in income of £800 in 1937 was attributed to losses sustained in the conversion of War Loan stocks coupled with a reduction in the value of the portfolio of investments, smaller subscriptions, and fewer donations. Expenditure continued to exceed income during the difficult war years, when many school activities were necessarily curtailed, but these losses were underwritten by assets which amounted to £55,610 in 1944, of which nearly £6,000 was accounted for by freehold land and buildings. The Schools were able to obtain some funds by means of joint Flag Days with other charities, permission for which was not easily obtained from the Watch Committee. A flag day in 1941 raised the handsome sum of £460, but, despite this form of assistance, operating losses for the two schools of £2,978 and £1.957 were incurred in 1944 and 1945 respectively. By this time there were no ordinary subscribers to the Charity.

In the first 30 years of the existence of the School in the eighteenth century several small legacies amounting in total to £500 were left to the Charity. Two hundred and fifty years later funds from these legacies were held in stocks valued at £530 and were yielding a total income of £18, an example of over-cautious financial management which had failed to reflect a sixty-fold fall in the value of money.

The position of the institution changed with the passing of the 1944 Education Act because the School was refused categorisation as a primary, secondary or boarding school and its main purpose as an educational establishment was at an end. Furthermore it was forecast that, with the introduction of Family Allowances in a forthcoming National Health Act, the numbers of children applying to enter the Schools would decline. Applications for admission to the Blue Coat School were suspended in June 1946 and it was decided by the Governors to close down the educational facilities at the end of 1946 and transfer the children to Park Grove Senior and Junior Schools in the New Year. The Schools would then become hostels rather than educational establishments. Soon afterwards the Governors reviewed the adequacy of funds to run separate hostels for boys and girls, and to meet the costs of bringing both sets of buildings up to modern standards. They decided, in February 1947, to close down the Blue Coat School at the end of the summer term when the boys were to be dispersed to their homes or to other institutions. The decision was received with mixed feelings by many friends of the institution, some of whom thought the closing down of the hostel accommodation for the boys was too abrupt.

Insufficient time had elapsed for the preparation of some form of commemoration of the Old Boys who had served in the Second World War and the whereabouts of items from the School museum and other mementoes are uncertain.

The Amos family stayed on at the School whilst Mr Amos prepared to take up an appointment at Harrogate but he died in December 1947 before he could take up his new post.

St Anthony's Hall was closed and those premises around the Hall which were owned by the charity were sold to York Corporation in February 1948 for £9000. Each side bore its own costs on condition that the Corporation abandoned its claim for severance and re-instatement.

It was the original intention of the Corporation to use part of the premises as a Day Continuation School linked with the Technical College in Clifford Street and it was also proposed to assign the Headmaster's flat to the caretaker of the Hall, to make spare rooms available for meetings and to open the premises to the public. During subsequent renovations 20 wooden spinning tops, probably whittled out by the boys a century earlier, and some shoe buckles, were found under the floor boards.

The recently formed York Civic Trust put forward a successful alternative proposal for the buildings to be used as a repository for the records of the Northern Province of the Church of England. The Academic Development Committee, the forerunner of York University, had already made these documents available for study at a series of Summer Schools. The buildings were converted with the assistance of grants from the Pilgrim Trust and the trustees of the late William Borthwick of Bridlington, and the premises were formally opened as The Borthwick Institute of Historical Research by the Princess Royal on 15 May 1953. The Institute, which is now an integral part of the University of York, includes a library and an expanding range of historical material including, fittingly, the records of the Blue Coat and Grey Coat Schools and St Stephen's Home.

In conclusion it is appropriate to quote Robert Davies, a local solicitor, who wrote in 1869 'During the long existence of this excellent charity it has never failed to experience the liberal support and excite the warm sympathy of those who have been the successors of its original founders.

B. THE GREY COAT SCHOOL
1705-1983

CHAPTER IV

1705-1783
High hopes followed by child labour

FIVE MONTHS AFTER THE OPENING of the Blue Coat School for Boys a similar institution for twenty girls was opened on October 29 1705, the day of St Simon and St Jude. Prebendary Bradley was the first secretary of the mainly female organising Committee and, in a sermon preached in the early days, he indicated that the object of the foundation was to provide a wholesome and pious education. He added that care would be taken to teach the children not only to say, but also to understand, their catechism. The girls were to be lodged, fed, taught, and clothed by subscription in the same manner as the boys. There was no mention at this stage of any intention to provide the girls with industrial training.

The school may have derived its name from the Gray Coat Hospital, or School of St Margaret's, in Tothill-side, Westminster. The first premises were at the bottom of Marygate on the west side of a lane leading to Almery Garth. Mistress Frances Thornhill, a devout lady, was credited with initiating this venture with a promise of a subscription of £5 annually. She enlisted the support of Mrs Sharp, the wife of the Archbishop, and the Hon. Lady Mary Fenwick the widow of Sir John Fenwick who was beheaded on the instructions of Cromwell during the Commonwealth.

Girls were entered for places in the School by their parents under penalty of £10, with a bondsman's security, for their good behaviour. Children who behaved badly could be brought before the Lord Mayor.

After some years the control of the School passed from Mrs Thornhill, the treasurer and sole manager to the Gentlemen's Committee which administered the Blue Coat School. This committee handed over the day to day running of the girls' school to a Master and Mistress who were paid a per capita fee for feeding and clothing the girls, including the provision of a cloak apiece. They were required to teach the girls to write, sew, knit and spin worsted. This contract arrangement gave rise to two opportunities for abuse, the first by skimping on food and clothing, and the second by contracting out the labour of the girls for the financial benefit of the Master and Mistress. The educational objects of the school soon became diluted under this latter arrangement.

Despite these shortcomings Mrs Bramforth, the mistress of the School between 1724 and 1754, was given ten guineas on her retirement for her fidelity and service and great care as Mistress of the girls.

One of her successors, Margaret Wolstenholme, lodged the girls in her own house and two of the girls acted as her domestic servants. She was allowed twenty shillings a year to provide the pupils with roast beef and 'plump' pudding at Christmas, Easter and Whitsuntide. In 1776 her husband, the joint Master of the Boys' and Girls' schools, was ordered to provide a proper bathing tub for the girls. This was on medical advice as a contribution to their personal hygiene. This facility was extended two years later when a workman was paid half a crown to clean out a well at the Manor Shore to provide cold baths for the children. The master was also instructed to provide forks, which were coming into general use, together with table knives. He supplied new cloaks in 1772 which were not replaced until 1809, a remarkable life for the textile employed which was a napped fabric called Blue Frizo. A cordwainer provided each girl with three pairs of shoes

Most of the girls were apprenticed into domestic service at varying ages with one working for a spinster and washerwoman, another for a widow and 'pastry' cook, a third was apprenticed at the late age of seventeen years and a fourth at eleven years old. One girl was apprenticed as a housemaid to John Camidge, the organist at St Michael-le-Belfrey Church. A Kirk Leatham farmer took four girls and eleven Blue Coat boys as apprentices in a two year period between 1777 and 1778. During their four year period of servitude the girls received an allowance for clothes from their employer on a sliding scale increasing from twenty shillings in the first year to fifty shillings in the final year. On satisfactory completion of their apprenticeships the girls received a gift of £3 from the School.

There were usually more applications from potential employers than girls for placement but in 1771 handbills were printed in York indicating that seven girls were awaiting suitable vacancies. These girls were available for apprenticeship with applicants who were approved by the Gentlemen's committee.

Three years later the following advertisement appeared in both the York Chronicle and York Courant under the heading 'Charity Girls':

> There are now at the Charity School in Marygate near the City several strong and healthy girls fit to be put out to respectable farmers and housekeepers. Mr Wolstenholme the Master will satisfy any enquiries.

One reason for inserting these advertisements was the competition for placements from similar establishments in the area including Ackworth School which, from 1757 - 1773, was an outstation of the London Foundling Hospital. Ackworth once sent out 166 children for apprenticeship in a single day, a scale of placement which gave little opportunity for vetting potential employers.

A different career opportunity for the girls opened up when John Lund, a local craftsman, offered to teach hardwood turning and trinket making (then known as toy making) to two girls still at the School. At the other end of the school cycle new entrants were required to confirm that they had had smallpox.

The capital funds available to the ruling Gentlemen's Committee, (usually known simply as the 'Gentlemen') were enhanced significantly in 1773 following a series of bequests to the two Charity Schools by William Haughton an eccentric Dancing

Front entrance, Grey Coat School, Monkgate.

Master. The initial bequest was £2,000 with a residuary interest in further large sums. The separate funds of the Blue Coat and Grey Coat schools had been merged some twenty years earlier.

It seems probable that some of the Haughton bequests were used to finance the transfer of the School to premises in Monkgate as a replacement for the decaying property in Marygate. The house and gardens in Monkgate were bought from Luke Farrar for £500 with a similar sum being spent on alterations and additions. Conditions were described as cold and spartan in the Monkgate premises and girls who suffered from chilblains were required to bathe their feet and ankles in cold water.

The new site extended from Monkgate to the Groves and was sufficiently extensive to provide space in the future for the Blue Coat School – a development which never materialised. The Monkgate buildings were partly hidden from the street by a high brick wall through which folding doors opened into a spacious courtyard. This area was subsequently transformed into a pleasant garden. The ground floor of the schoolhouse consisted of spinning and sewing rooms, and a flight of stone steps led up to the first floor. This contained a dormitory with eighteen iron bedsteads for two girls to each bed. Nearby was sleeping accommodation for the schoolmistress who remained constantly with her pupils. Other premises included a range of outbuildings and an adjacent matron's apartment which contained a kitchen and lodging rooms.

CHAPTER V

The Grey Coat School 1783-1850 A major reform by the ladies

THE SUB-CONTRACTING METHOD OF operating the Grey Coat school was brought to an end by a chain of events originating in a manufactory based in St Andrewgate churchyard which was operated by a Mr Hooker. This enterprise was described as a hop-bag manufactory which produced hemp sacking, harding, wool sheeting and fine sacking for upholsterers. It employed 60 children of both sexes in very unsatisfactory working and moral conditions and was the largest single employer of labour in York in 1783.

The conditions at Mr Hooker's establishment came to the notice of a group of ladies with charitable interests including Mrs Faith Gray, Lady Anderson, Miss Swainston and Mrs Catherine Cappe (formerly Miss Harrison). The group attempted to set up a school at which children employed by Hooker could receive some education in the evenings and be encouraged to attend Church on Sundays. This venture failed, partly because the children were too tired after their long working day to benefit from such assistance, and partly because the scheme still left them exposed to the moral dangers of the manufactory.

The ladies re-thought their approach and set up a Spinning School to employ 22 children full-time, subject to the consent of their parents. Comprehensive rules were drawn up for the operation of the School under the supervision of a matron who worked under the close control of a Ladies' Committee. A Knitting School on similar principles was established for younger children. The ladies were inspired by a published quotation 'Let the poor be well

YORK CHILDREN'S TRUST

INCORPORATING THE BLUE & GREY COAT SCHOOLS
and ST. STEPHEN'S
(Registered Charity No. 222279)

with compliments

H G SHERRIFF - Clerk/Treasurer
34 Lucombe Way, New Earswick, York YO32 4DS

Telephone York 750705

Mrs Catherine Cappe, 1744-1821.

educated and the differences in conduct and understanding will repay Society for the trouble they undertake'.

The rules and methods of working were in some respects similar to those introduced at the Greenwich Charity School earlier in the century. Mrs Cappe, the wife of a Unitarian minister, circulated details of her scheme widely in response to requests for this information from many parts of the country. Consequently it is possible that the manner in which the Spinning School was organised and operated may have had a beneficial influence on similar institutions elsewhere. Mrs Cappe published accounts of the project in the Monthly Magazine and in her book 'An Account of Two Charity Schools for the Education of Girls and of a Female friendly Society in York' which was published in 1799. The Spinning School at 28 St Andrewgate closed down in 1858 and its surplus funds of £580 were transferred to the Grey Coat School.

Mrs Cappe had been aware of the reputation of the Grey Coat School from about 1780 onwards. Whereas the Blue Coat School was regarded as a useful institution, which was on the whole well-conducted, it seemed that very few of the girls from the Grey Coat School turned out well. Many of them were sickly, they were remarkably low of stature and their whole appearance was very unfavourable. Some of the past pupils had drifted into prostitution.

The early success of the Spinning School ventures came to the notice of the Gentlemen, two of whom invited Mrs Cappe and several friends, known collectively as the 'Ladies', to give their opinion regarding the regulations and methods of working necessary to put the Grey Coat School on a sound footing. The Ladies submitted a paper setting out appropriate ends and objects applicable to a Charity School for Girls, which found favour with the Gentlemen and led to the Ladies being invited to visit the School. There they found the thirty children generally diseased, both in body and mind, their appearance sickly and dejected, their ignorance extreme, and – as described by the Master and Mistress – their moral depravity truly deplorable.

These sorts of girls, and parish apprentices, could only be placed with the poorer types of employers who taught them little of the craft of the housewife. Relationships between female apprentices and employers were usually poor and it was common for the girls to be in moral danger. Mrs Cappe recognized the hazards of these apprenticeship arrangements and campaigned locally, and in a wider sphere, for such schemes to be discontinued. She argued that young girls in their early teens should not be placed under the absolute control of masters or mistresses and that such girls should remain at the School until they had attained more mature years. She recommended that, on leaving the School, the girls should be employed as wage earners without the constraints of apprenticeship conditions.

The Ladies proceeded cautiously with their recommendations in order not to generate opposition and, as a first step, recommended the appointment of two assistant teachers, one for the Sewing Room and the other to teach sewing, knitting and line (flax) spinning.

Up to that time the Master and Mistress could employ the girls as best suited their convenience and had the financial benefit of their labour. As a first step in reducing the control of a recently appointed husband and wife team the wages of the assistant teachers were paid by the Gentlemen.

The Ladies began to make almost daily visits to the School and the benefits of the modest changes which they had proposed soon became apparent. The Ladies next proposed two far reaching changes in the operation of the School, namely the cessation of the practice of boarding the girls with the Master and Mistress, and the abandonment of the the practice of putting out girls of any age as apprentices. These fundamental changes were not at that stage acceptable to the Gentlemen.

Within four months it became obvious that the Master was not suited to his post and the Mistress was mentally deranged, so the Gentlemen agreed to the appointment of a Matron in October 1786. The Ladies were given power to follow the dictates of their own judgment in respect of the regulation of the girls whilst they remained in the School, at the time of their leaving, and in their subsequent deployment. Apprenticeships were abandoned to avoid girls in their early teens being placed in moral danger when they left the control of the School.

The Ladies formed themselves into the Ladies' Committee and elected sub-committees to supervise school books and expenditure, clothing, supplies of wool for spinning and School Visitors. The latter system of inspecting Visitors was to continue throughout the life of the Grey Coat School.

It was decided that, in future, provisions and other household expenses would be paid for out of the funds of the Charity instead of by per capita payments to the Master and Mistress.

The cost of maintaining girls in the School in 1786 was £10 per head per annum made up as follows:

	£. s. d.
Clothing and household linen	1. 19. 6.
Shoes	17. 0.
Food	5. 0. 0.
Staff salaries	1. 11. 0.
Apothecaries' bills	2. 0.
Coal, soap, candles etc.	10. 6.
Total	10. 0. 0.

The weekly rations of the girls included 11 pints of skimmed milk – some of which was set out with bread for breakfast, 22 ounces of meat which was served thrice weekly and 4 lbs. of bread flour. Bread was available in unlimited quantities at any time of the day. Boiled milk thickened with oatmeal was provided for breakfast in the winter. Tea, sugar, butter and eggs were not included in the diet.

As a first step in providing better educational facilities the Ladies engaged a writing master in 1786. He was paid eight guineas a year to teach the girls to write and cast accounts.

From 1794 the girls were allowed to sit down to their dinners to make for a more refreshing meal after they had been on their legs spinning for six or seven hours. To compensate for the heavy workload holidays were long and the specified hours of play were not intruded upon. Work ceased at six o'clock in the evening whether tasks were finished or not. By 1804 the girls were allowed a candle in the School from dark until bed time during the six winter months. It was considered improper for the girls to go out on summer Assize Days, which tended to be rowdy, and they were given a pint of gooseberries instead.

The children were clothed by the School on a scale related to their work output. To qualify for a basic set of clothing they were required to spin six hanks of yarn a day, whilst those who completed seven hanks daily for one year were provided with stays and awarded a full outfit of clothing. Good spinners could earn up to 2s.8d. per week and those who spun one pound of wool to 40 hanks or more received special gifts such as a shawl, a Barcelona handkerchief, a white apron or occasionally a book.

Amongst other improvements introduced by the Ladies was the provision of an outfit of clothes when girls were placed in service by the school. This outfit belonged to the school and could be withdrawn temporarily or permanently if the girl left her position. School leavers were also given a Bible, a Book of Common Prayer and a copy of 'Pilgrim's Progress'.

In later years emphasis was placed on encouraging girls to stay in their first job by providing modest rewards. Gifts of print dresses were made to girls who earned certificates for good behaviour and completed one year of service with their employers. Girls who stayed with the same employer for three years received a book.

Mrs Bedingfield was engaged in 1790 to visit the School frequently at 6 a.m. to see that the girls and mistresses were down from the dormitories, and again at 9 p.m. to confirm that each girl was in her proper bed wearing her night cap.

The new regime continued severe penalties for persistent misbehaviour. For instance, girls who absented themselves without leave from the Matron were required to wear special clogs and a jacket bearing a red 'R' for one day. This was the penalty for a first offence. Pupils committing a second transgression were additionally handcuffed for a day; a third offence resulted in the youngster being locked in a garret for three days on a diet of bread and water wearing handcuffs to prevent her hurting herself. Disobedient noisy children were controlled by means of half a handkerchief tied across the mouth. Other offenders were required to go on their knees to seek a pardon from members of the staff and members of the Ladies' Committee and, in the case of one girl, 'to have no apple pie at the Feast on Thursday next'. As late as 1868 a girl responsible for a series of thefts and untruths was whipped in front of the whole school with her parents present

The girls were required to pay a forfeit for items lost, torn, broken or out of place. The penalties for goods mislaid included sixpence for stays, a penny for a handkerchief or a dustpan, and a half penny for a gown.

As early as 1794 the prices paid by agents for spinning wool were falling as a consequence of the introduction of machine spinning of yarn. The spinning activities of the School fell away abruptly in 1806 with the expansion of the machine spinning of wool in the manufactories. The only work available for the twenty spinners consisted of limited quantities of worsted to be used by stocking knitters. The girls were also taught to spin line (flax) but, despite this new venture, all spinning activities had ceased at the School by 1837.

After the introduction of the reforms proposed by Mrs Cappe and her friends the School was run by a Committee of seven Ladies chosen by the subscribers. This Committee was subject to the general supervision of the Gentlemen. The Ladies jealously guarded, throughout the life of the School, their right to superintend the food and clothing of the girls and to appoint and dismiss staff. Friction between the Ladies and Gentlemen arose sometimes during times of financial stringency, or after controversial staff appointments. On these occasions the Gentlemen faced accusations of over-riding the Ladies and conciliatory joint meetings were called to resolve the disputes. Piquancy was added to the situation when husbands and wives were concurrent members of the respective committees.

The disciplinary measures taken over by the Ladies from the earlier regime did not resolve the problem of threats and abusive conduct towards mistresses on the part of parents and friends of the girls, and four girls were expelled in 1822. The Ladies Committee concluded that this problem stemmed from an insufficient use by the mistresses of the powers of correction available to them for dealing with the increased number of pupils which had by now risen to 46.

The 1820s were a period of pupil disruption and indiscipline in the girls' school, and also in the boys' school. By 1828 the girls' school was reported to be in a state of insubordination and eleven girls were expelled for misconduct, including ten in one batch. A further nine girls were expelled in 1829 and the management committee of the boys' school was called upon to assist the Ladies in effecting improvements in the management of the female institution.

After a review of the disciplinary problems of both schools it was concluded that the admission procedures were at fault and that insufficient care had been paid for many years with regard to the backgrounds and the medical records of successful applicants, and to the marital status of their parents. Accordingly in 1829 a twenty-one member annually-elected Committee (the Annual Committee) was established to examine all candidates for admission and to ensure that health and other requirements were met.

It was re-affirmed that parents and guardians were required to relinquish the entire control and management of the children during their stay at the School. The Ladies also had the power to put the children out to household service at 15 years of age.

As in the boys' school the disciplinary problems in the 1820s did not prevent the running cost of the girls' school being successfully reduced. The annual cost of feeding and clothing the girls fell from £13 in 1821 to £9 in 1830. Changes introduced in 1848 included the substitution of plates for platters and the less popular introduction of scholastic examinations for the girls. Places in domestic service were scarce at this time but the Gentlemen took a hard line and required the Ladies to be peremptory in dismissing unemployed girls from the School at the age of 15 if no housework could be found for them in the institution.

The Ladies clearly recognised that the calibre of the matron was the main factor in the successful operation of the school. The qualities sought in a matron in mid-century were defined as membership of the Church of England combined with the possession of decided piety and sound judgement. Candidates for the job were required to be conversant with household affairs, capable of educating the children and training them for domestic service.

Despite this awareness of the required qualities the Grey Coat school, unlike the Blue Coat School, did not succeed in recruiting any outstanding matron or school mistress in the nineteenth century.

CHAPTER VI

The Grey Coat School 1850-1921
The gradual refinement of Victorian values

IN A SURPRISING RELINQUISHMENT of responsibility the Ladies expressed the view in 1853 that the control of expenditure, accounts and general business of the Grey Coat School had not been well conducted under their supervision. The Ladies accordingly handed over responsibility for these matters to the Gentlemen and decided that in the future they would confine their activities to scrutinising bills for payment, inspecting the clothing of the children, providing a formal Visiting service and examining applications for admission to the School. The School bills amounted to about £150 per month including £30 for flour, £20 for meat and £13 for milk. Payments were made in most months to the Christian Knowledge Society for books which were either given to school leavers or used in the school room.

In later years the business of the sub-committee which approved bills for payment, and placed the contract for the once-yearly cleaning of the school, was sometimes transacted by a single attender at the regular quarterly meetings. Attendance at Annual Meetings was also sparse and in several years no subscribers attended these meetings.

The children's clothing requirements were supervised by a separate sub-committee which was involved in the abolition in 1881 of a number of traditional items of dress including straw bonnets, frilled caps, muslin aprons and tippets. The traditional headgear was discarded in order to make the girls less conspicuous when they were away from the School. This was a move away from the traditional approach that both out of school activities, and school uniforms, should be as eye-catching as possible in order to engender financial support from the general public for the two Charity Schools.

The School attempted to keep in touch with its old scholars, particularly in the first few years after they had left the institution, by means of an Old Scholars' Day which was introduced in 1856. This was described as 'An Annual Tea Drinking for the girls in service'. Amongst the 40 Old Scholars attending the reunion in 1899 was Mrs Bilborough who had entered a very different School some 86 years earlier in 1813.

Minor improvements were made in the school facilities in the early 1860s including the provision of a sick room and also a sitting room for the matron. A more extensive series of changes was initiated in 1867 after the Gentlemen had concluded that the school premises were ill-suited for their intended purpose. It was decided to retain the existing schoolroom and dormitory and pull down the remainder of the buildings on the site. The school was transferred to a large house in Osbaldwick for six months whilst the building operations were in progress.

This improvement in residential facilities at Monkgate, at a cost of £2,000, was funded by a bequest from Dr Beckwith. It was planned to increase the number of girls in residence to 50 but, in the event, the highest number ever accommodated was 44 between 1872 and 1874. Shortage of income for both schools precluded a further expansion in pupil numbers.

In 1868 Robert Davies, the local historian, gave 400 copies of his 'History of St Anthony's Hall' to be sold in aid of the alterations at Monkgate. He was associated with Schools for 54 years as a valued member of the Gentlemen's Committee.

The health of the girls gave some cause for concern in the late 1870s and girls with delicate constitutions were required to wear flannel vests. Two girls were sent to the Sea Bathing Infirmary at Scarborough under the ticket system whereby subscribers were entitled to send their nominees for treatment. Other girls were sent to a convalescent home at Appleton to recuperate from sickness.

Meanwhile girls in normal health typically enjoyed a day trip to Bridlington and a day on a farm at Flaxton. In order to ensure that the girls enjoyed plenty of exercise and fresh air they were provided with skipping ropes and hoops. They were also taken out for walks on two afternoons and one morning a week.

The deaths of two girls were attributed tersely to 'decline' or delicate health. Following the deaths of three other girls from consumption, improvements were made to the premises in 1877. Ventilation in the dormitory was enhanced, stone floors in the schoolroom were replaced by boards and an improved grate was added to the fireplace. Single beds for the girls were introduced over a three year period with Committee members contributing to the cost of purchase of the last few beds. A further improvement in amenities and personal privacy took place when the communal bath was replaced by five separate baths. Six water closets were introduced at the turn of the century.

The educational side of the school was unsatisfactory and the school teacher resigned in 1880 because she could not control the girls. Two years earlier some of the older girls were described as unusually dull and taking little part in the Annual examination. Both the education and domestic control of the girls were hampered by the long standing lack of continuity in the staffing of the School. For example, in the three year period between 1879 and 1881, one matron resigned through ill-health, her replacement soon departed and a third appointment was made. One schoolmistress resigned, two others went away in quick succession and a fourth left to get married.

In an attempt to ease some of these problems the general monitresses, drawn from the older girls, were replaced by a more mature sub-matron. The supervisory visiting arrangements were strengthened in 1881 so that six subscribers were nominated each quarter to visit the school in pairs alongside Committee members on their monthly visitations. The visitors were required to record their observations in a book and soon commented that they had found the school buildings dirty and unswept.

The daily milk allowance of the girls was increased from one pint to one and a half pints a day in 1880 because the diet was considered to be insufficiently nourishing. As a result of a further review in 1882 it was concluded that the diet of the girls was below the level of comparable institutions and other changes were gradually introduced. In the following year it was agreed to serve fish one day a week, 20lbs being the quantity required for the entire School. Later the same year an extra 14lbs of butchers' meat and 4lbs of dripping were added to the weekly shopping list. Sixteen years later, soon after the turn of the century, it was agreed to increase the vegetable diet of the girls and legs of mutton were introduced to the menu. Children were given the choice of oatmeal porridge and treacle, or milk and bread, for breakfast in the winter months.

Attention was focussed on the suitability of Grey Coat girls as employees who would stay for a reasonable period in their first posts after leaving School. In the 1880s cards were displayed in the school showing the names of leavers and the length of time they had continued in their first job. Girls received a gift of £1 if they had conducted themselves in a thoroughly satisfactory manner for two or three years after leaving the School. This gift was entirely at the discretion of the Ladies but other relatively minor expenses, for the Annual Treat in the form of a day trip to Scarborough, and for token prizes to children still in the School, (amounting in total to about £3), required the approval of the Gentlemen. These token prizes were known collectively as the Midsummer Awards.

The School drew the majority of its intake of about six to ten girls a year from the City of York but the Gentlemen conceded that girls could be admitted from outlying villages if at least three permanent subscribers to the School lived in the vicinity. Girls from Nether Poppleton, Marston Moor and Sutton on Derwent were admitted under this arrangement. In order to widen the interests and skills of the older girls a course of 12 cookery lessons, subsequently extended to 20 lessons, was conducted by a teacher from the National School of Cookery in York.

The Gentlemen continued to exercise close control of the School and sometimes ignored suggestions from the Ladies. The latter unsuccessfully recommended that the holidays granted on the first Thursday in each month should be restricted to a quarterly basis. It was thought that the girls became unsettled and exposed to evil influences, which were difficult to correct, by visiting their homes so frequently. At this time the school holidays consisted of two days at Easter, nineteen days in late July, and eleven days at Christmas.

Another unsuccessful recommendation concerned the introduction of drill lessons to correct stooping postures and encourage better deportment. This recommendation was eventually accepted some years later when the Ladies agreed to pay for the services of a drill sergeant.

The male dominance of the management of the School continued into the next century when, in a short-lived rule change in 1903, it was decided that the members of the Ladies' Committee should be elected by the Gentlemen rather than by the general body of subscribers. This ruling was overturned in the following year when it was decided that seven or more ladies should be chosen by the annual meeting of subscribers to regulate the affairs of the girls' school, subject to the supervision of the Gentlemen. The Ladies, with a quorum of three, had power to examine female candidates for admission, regulate the education, maintenance, and clothing of the girls and confirm the expulsion of girls from the School. With a quorum of five they could appoint and dismiss the Matron and Mistress. Complaints were received from several employers in 1884 that girls recruited from the School were slow and incompetent. After an investigation it was concluded that the schoolroom was being conducted satisfactorily but that a matron was needed who could exercise more moral control and influence on the girls. A new Matron, Miss Finch, was appointed in 1885 with these requirements in mind.

One of her first changes was to order new sets of stays for the girls. This was followed by replacements for the cloaks which had been in use for fifteen years. The girls were less than fully provided with underwear by modern standards and it was recommended that in future all the 44 girls in the School should be provided with drawers made from calico. During the First World war flannel petticoats were discarded and serge knickers were introduced as standard wear for upwards of the next fifty years.

The teaching staff of one schoolmistress was augmented soon afterwards by a pupil teacher. The appointee was given her clothing and pocket money of £2 per annum. Her successors received £4 in 1902, increasing to £5 for the second year in the job. A system of paid monitresses for domestic work, recruited from the older girls, had been in operation for some years, but this form of supplementary help did not significantly alleviate understaffing problems. The continuing education of these monitresses improved from around 1905 when they were allowed to attend evening classes in book-keeping, dressmaking and other subjects

The School acquired nearly 2,500 square feet of adjacent garden, previously owned by Mr Earle, in 1825 at a cost of £442. The school re-possessed the sub-let portion of this garden area in 1887 to provide additional playground accommodation. The newly available area was laid out with a grass central area surrounded by an asphalt path and a six foot cultivated border. The Ladies agreed to pay for apple trees to be planted round the lawn.

In the past parents and friends had been allowed to visit girls at the School on Saturday afternoons on an unrestricted basis. This was found to have a disturbing effect on the girls and was also alleged to give rise to much gossip and confusion. In 1887 a rule was introduced forbidding such visits unless approved by the Matron or Ladies Committee for special reasons.

In the early 1890s Alderman Close, later a Lord Mayor of York, became a generous benefactor to the girls in parallel with his generosity to the boys. For several years he entertained the children at his home, the 'Hollies' on Tadcaster Road, transporting them there in brakes. The girls were provided with tea, together with five shillings for depositing in their personal bank accounts, and a further shilling for pocket money. This generous gesture was taken over by J.P.Bulmer for 3 years until his death. Alderman Close also provided a sum of £5 per annum to employ a cookery teacher and, when a suitable teacher could not be found, transferred the payment to a woman to teach the girls pattern-cutting, and the making up of garments, so that the pupils could provide their own clothing. This annual payment for tuition was transferred to a teacher of gymnastics in 1898.

The children received regular supplies of gifts and pocket money from other sources including one shilling apiece at Christmas from a legacy left by Alderman Wilson in 1821, a sixpence and an orange after the annual visit to the Mansion House, and a token prize for every girl at the annual prize giving.

A shortage of applicants for admission to the School occurred in 1896, several years earlier than a similar situation in the boys' school. This was an unusual turn of events, and clergymen and members of the Committees were asked to seek out orphans or friendless children and bring them forward as candidates for admission.

The girls participated in the Golden and Diamond Jubilee celebrations for Queen Victoria in 1887 and 1897 with tea parties, outdoor games, and musical entertainments on Bootham Field. On both occasions the girls were taken in the evenings to see the illuminations and the school was given a piano as a Diamond Jubilee gift. Later in the Jubilee summer of 1897, after the customary annual treat to Scarborough, the girls were taken in brakes to Bishopthorpe Palace to be entertained by Archbishop and Mrs Maclagan.

At this time the joint secretaries of the Ladies' Committee were Miss Elizabeth Gray, whose family had been associated with the school since the 1780s and Mrs Jane Shann, wife of a previous Medical Officer and mother of a future Medical Officer of the School. Mrs Shann retired in 1898 after helping the School for 50 years as a member, and latterly secretary, of the Ladies' Committee

Three girls were regularly assigned to the Blue Coat School to help with housekeeping tasks, a long standing arrangement which dated back to the middle of the eighteenth century. The Grey Coat School also provided a shirt making and shirt repairing service for the boys. When the numbers of pupils increased at St Anthony's Hall there was a consequent increase in the workload falling on the girls, who were also responsible for repairing their own clothes. The shirt repairing commitment became increasingly burdensome during the 1890s, particularly when clothes were required to be put in good order before holiday periods, and in consequence an additional Sewing Mistress was appointed in 1897. The problem continued because of the difficulty in accommodating the mental education of the children alongside the sewing commitment, which occupied one third of the total classroom hours.

The possibility of obtaining statutory grant aid was mooted and led to an official review by the Inspectorate of Schools. This visit was followed by a favourable report in which it was recommended that the introduction of a second school mistress was a necessary pre-requisite for grant aid from the State for the School. A subsequent proposal to seek grant-aided status was lost by one vote at a quarterly meeting of the Gentlemen and the existing educational system was retained. In subsequent years School Visitors drawn from the subscribers began to recommend the transfer of the children to public elementary schools.

The range of the curriculum is illustrated by the programme for the annual examination in 1900, which was conducted in public. The examiners consisted of two clergymen and a teacher and the topics included Old and New Testament texts, a carol, a song, a recitation (Horatius), history (the Tudors) and geography (Ireland and India). Written elements included arithmetic, composition and dictation. An H.M.I. attended in an unofficial capacity and expressed full satisfaction with the teaching in the school room. At subsequent annual public examinations the girls displayed examples of bread, cakes and puddings which they had cooked.

The girls were relieved of some of their heavier house-cleaning chores by the engagement of a charwoman who subsequently received a pension of 6d per week from each member of the Ladies' Committee. Around that time the Directors took the opportunity to reiterate the rule that no paid work should be undertaken in the School by members of the Permanent Committee – many of whom were local businessmen.

The name of a well-known local architect, Walter Brierley, appeared in the minutes in 1903 when approval was given to his plans for the construction of a cloakroom created by a re-arrangement of the existing pantry and bakehouse facilities. A modern cooking range and an improved type of hot water apparatus followed some years later.

The Charity Schools took part in an extensive programme to celebrate the bi-centenary of the institutions in 1905. A souvenir booklet was produced and gatherings organised of old scholars who presented commemorative plaques and framed photographs to both Schools. The children from the Schools occupied the choir at a service in the Minster; they provided entertainments and were themselves entertained. An Open day was held when members of the general public could view the Schools.

The annual visit to Scarborough by the older girls was replaced in 1908 by a week long visit by each of two groups to a furnished cottage at Howsham, loaned by Miss Toynbee. Another notable event in the same year was the departure of a girl called Hields to Canada under an emigration scheme organised by the Girls' Friendly Society. The Ladies paid for her passage and travelling outfit. Three years later E.M. West emigrated to New Zealand under the auspices of the same Society. Despite the extensive scale of emigration from the United Kingdom to the Empire in the latter part of the nineteenth and early part of the twentieth century these are the only recorded examples of children from the Charity Schools being involved.

A punishment book was introduced in 1907 and submitted quarterly to the Gentlemen for their scrutiny. An early entry discloses that a group of eight girls was caned together for dirty habits. A ninth pupil, who saw this as an occasion for mirth, received a similar punishment. Other naughty children were sent to bed on half holidays. Ten offenders were caned in 1912 and sixteen in the peak year of 1918. Another form of punishment was recorded in 1912 when four residents were placed on a bread and water diet for two days as punishment for running away or insubordination. Several small girls were caned in 1917 for cheating and deceit and in 1919 three were whipped for depraved habits. The last caning took place in 1920 and the book ended in 1925.

An emergency sub-committee was available to deal with serious misdemeanours. The Ladies deprecated the use of a cane and, taking an understanding view of carelessness and displays of temper, they recommended that girls should not pay for the resulting losses and breakages out of their own money but should be punished by other means.

Another recording system was introduced in 1908 in the form of a Matron's Log Book which was required to comply with a new code for schools receiving statutory Annual Grants. Early entries gave an indication of the range of leisure activities provided for the girls. The period from 1908 to 1910 saw the introduction of a Band of Hope (a temperance organisation) and visits by train to Warthill to gather blackberries and to Hazelbush Woods. In 1908 the girls attended a Chrysanthemum show in York, an exhibition of pictures at South Bank Adult School and an animated picture show. In the following year the older girls took part in a Girls Friendly Society Class and Band of Hope meetings at St Michael-le-Belfrey. They attended a Missionary meeting at St William's College, enjoyed an Annual Treat to Scarborough, toured the York Pageant, went by steamer to Naburn and took a picnic to fields at the farm of Mrs Barstow at Warthill. They saw an early review of Boy Scouts, went blackberrying, listened to a talk on Japan, visited two flower shows, gave a tea party for their brothers and sisters and were themselves entertained at seasonal parties.

In 1910 several older girls listened to the proclamation of King George V, attended the funeral service for King Edward VII and the Military Sunday Service in the Minster, and participated in a picnic at Osbaldwick on Empire Day (May 24th). They were given seats at the Musical Festival and visited a Menagerie. They also sailed up the Ouse on the 'River King' to a tea party at the Red House, Moor Monkton and attended a Picture Show at Victoria Hall. The girls were provided with a residential holiday in a cottage at Whixley which was rented for a fortnight. In the following year the holiday was at Filey.

It was the practice at this time to board out girls who could not go home during the summer holidays at a cost of five shillings per head per week. In 1913 boarding places were found at Dunnington, Bolton Percy and Wentbridge Convalescent Home.

In a bid to ensure that the School met its commitment to support the girls in the early post-school years the document signed by parents or guardians when children entered the School was revised in 1912. Under the new arrangement the control of the Ladies over the girls' choice of occupation or employer was extended to one year after leaving the School. Since the early days of the School girls could not be removed without the consent of the appropriate Committee, a requirement which was re-introduced after two years of discussion in 1916. In cases where parents or friends breached this undertaking the Committee sought contributions, not always successfully, towards the cost of maintaining and clothing the child.

The First World War affected the School in a number of relatively minor ways. Because there was a risk of coastal bombardment, seaside holidays were replaced by holidays in the countryside. It was decided that in the event of an air raid warning the girls were to be brought down to the ground floor but they were only required to descend to the cellars if enemy aircraft were in the vicinity. The girls saw war pictures at the cinema, darkened their curtains against Zeppelin raids under the Defence of the Realm Act, heard a talk on happenings in a military hospital, bought National Savings certificates at a tank parked in the centre of York, were present at an entertainment for returned prisoners of war and finally attended the Armistice Day service in York Minister on November 11 1918. During the war-time years the School lawn was cut back by nine feet on each side in order to grow potatoes and some of the older girls assisted with the production of the crops. Other parts of the playground were taken over by the Army. Matron was instructed to conform as far as possible with food rationing regulations so long as this did not entail stinting the children of their diet, a task made easier by the allocation to the School of double the rations permitted for private households. An unexpected source of pocket money was the shilling apiece paid to girls for assisting matron to colour wash the kitchen and scullery areas. This supplemented the shilling which each girl had been receiving since 1911 on the birthday of William Richard Beckwith.

In 1917 the School was requested by the Soldiers' and Sailors' Family Association to admit, for the duration of the war, children of widowers on Active Service. For the first time in the history of the School payments were sought for the maintenance of such children but attempts to seek payments for other children already in the School met with only limited success. By 1920 most new entrants had one parent living and there were few orphans remaining in the School.

In 1919 it was agreed with some reluctance to comply with the new Fisher Act and place the School under Government inspection in order to qualify for a grant of £1 per pupil under the terms of Section 15 of the 1902 Education Act. Compliance with the requirements of the Act entailed little change in the running of the School except that records were required to be kept of school attendances and that a minimum attendance of 400 half days per annum was required for each child. The teaching posts became pensionable and the assistant teachers were required to be qualified.

CHAPTER VII
The Grey Coat School 1921-1945 The reluctant introduction of co-education

THE SCHOOL ENJOYED A PERIOD of freedom from staff changes for many years until July 1919 when both matron and headmistress announced their intentions to resign their posts. The Matron, Miss New, had completed 11 years service and the schoolmistress, Miss Watson, had spent 16 years with the School. In the event they both agreed to remain at the School for a further year after which replacements were found. The possibility of uniting the schoolrooms of the two Charity Schools was discussed, in conjunction with these changes of staff, but not pursued.

During an interregnum discipline deteriorated and control was only partly restored after the ringleader in insubordination had left the School. Stability was restored in the short term, and for many years to come, with the appointment in January 1921 of Miss Gladys Bazzard as Matron. Her salary was fixed at £80 per annum increasing to £90 after six months. Miss Bazzard was assisted by a sewing matron and a kitchen matron and actively supported by the Ladies who took a more active part in the management of the School.

In her first few months in the job Miss Bazzard replaced the traditional cloaks with grey coats and also acquired substantial supplies of materials to replace stockings, aprons and handkerchiefs. Amongst her many other tasks was the cutting of the girls' hair, with the resulting fringes prominent in many photographs.

A fresh proposal to send children to the local elementary school was ruled out because of the possibility that trust funds would be lost if the School ceased to be an educational institution. The Ladies objected to an amalgamation of the two Charity Schools mainly because of the likely loss of their control over both the appointment of teachers and the arrangement of the girls' timetables.

From 1920 onwards the maintenance of a small proportion of the girls was paid for by parents or guardians and the names of children admitted under this arrangement did not appear on the ballot papers for entry into the school. Two important, and unrelated changes in the Rules of the School were introduced in 1921. Firstly, the Ladies were offered two places on the main Committee responsible for the School and secondly, children could be admitted whilst awaiting election by the subscribers. This latter amendment overcame the problem of finding temporary accommodation for girls seeking admission.

In 1922 the School rented for the first time a house at Filey belonging to St Stephen's Home and continued the arrangement for many years. Twenty six scholars and two matrons formed the pioneering visiting party.

The Press report of the Annual Meeting in 1922 noted that prizes were awarded to the girls for good manners, darning, scrubbing, breadmaking, laundry work brass cleaning, perseverance, neatness, knitting, accuracy in learning collects, and hemstitching. It was announced that Edith Jennings had gained a scholarship to Queen Anne's School, an achievement which was celebrated by a holiday for her fellow pupils. Edith subsequently passed through teacher training and became an assistant teacher at Strensall.

In the early post-war years fund raising became a major activity for the Charity Schools with £300 raised by house-to-house collections in 1919. The daunting total of 20,000 fund-raising pamphlets was distributed in 1920 by old scholars and friends of the School.

To celebrate the wedding of the Duke and Duchess of York in April 1923 the girls attended a cinema show in the morning and games in the afternoon followed by tea paid for by the bridegroom. On the occasion of the wedding of the previous Duke of York in 1893 the girls had been given a 'good tea' and taken on a picnic to the Knavesmire.

Miss Bazzard with girls in traditional dress.

After several years of discussion the schooling of the boys and girls was finally combined at St Anthony's Hall in 1924 despite the continuing protests of the Ladies. The girls and boys sat on opposite sides of the classroom. Not unexpectedly there were ongoing criticisms by Miss Bazzard of the facilities provided for the girls under the new arrangements. The possibility of sending all the children to elementary schools was still a live issue because the Schools were short of income arising partly from a decline in the numbers of children whose maintenance was paid for by outside agencies and partly from a falling off in subscription income.

The new schooling arrangements were opposed by some supporters who contended that the main objective of the Schools should be to give needy children the benefit of institutional care as envisaged by the founders of the Schools. These opponents argued that the responsibility for financing the costs of the education of the children should be assumed by the local authority.

A restriction on the career prospects of the girls came to notice in 1928 when two pupils were refused permission to take examinations for the School of Commerce. The argument was put forward that the remuneration of a young female clerk was insufficient to enable the girls, neither of whom had a home, to be self supporting. Residential domestic service was judged to be a more suitable alternative as in the case of a girl who had recently left to be third housemaid at Bishopthorpe Palace. Another thirteen years were to pass before it was accepted that girls showing exceptional aptitude should be encouraged to pursue their bent.

The Ladies decided that too much time and energy was spent on scrubbing floors and Matron was instructed to arrange a reduction of this task by two thirds. At the same time the girls were relieved of the task of cleaning the windows at the rear of the house at fortnightly intervals. The floor cleaning commitment was not alleviated until the introduction of polished floors after another decade.

By 1925 57 boys and 22 girls were being taught in three classes, each in separate schoolrooms. Monthly educational tests were introduced and the scope of the annual examinations was increased. Girls remained in the classrooms until they reached the age of 14 after which they were taught domestic science for two years in the form of cooking, needlework, bedmaking and laundry work. The children were entered for outside competitions in which they gained first class certificates for Morris dancing and singing. Some girls joined the Girl Guides where they won a trophy for thrift and many proficiency badges. Swimming and organised games were added to the curriculum and the younger girls received domestic science training at an outside school.

The arrival of a new headmaster at the Bluecoat School was followed by the introduction of organised games for the girls and younger boys together with occasional school walks and visits to places of interest. Organised swimming lessons followed a few years later and poultry keeping and gardening were also added to the list of school activities. By 1936 the girls were attending classes in singing, folk dancing and physical fitness and were very successful in Yorkshire Folk Dancing competitions. The changes in personnel at the head of both schools were accompanied by an increase in Civic interest over the Christmas period. The schools were decorated more elaborately, the children sang carols for the Civic party and Christmas gifts for the girls were more numerous than in the past.

External events were reflected in the domestic life of the school when a larger gas cooker was installed to offset the coal shortage during the General Strike in 1926.

When Miss Elizabeth Gray resigned as honorary secretary of the Ladies Committee in 1930, after completing 32 years in the post, it was noted that she was the fifth generation of her family to have served the School as a Committee member. The family connection went back to the Mrs Gray who was the first chairman of the Woman's Committee in 1788.

Female participation in the management of the Schools was increased significantly and belatedly in 1932 when the main Committee of Gentlemen was reorganised as the Executive Committee. A combined House Committee was introduced for both Schools with women constituting 13 of its 18 members. All questions of food, clothing and internal management were assigned to the House Committee. Five of the the ten members of the Education Committee were women and the female Honorary Secretary represented the Ladies on the Finance Committee. The House Committee recommended, and the Executive Committee approved, applications for admission of children to the Schools. The Ladies Committee continued to function and met monthly at the Greycoat School to coordinate with the House Committee for that institution. The Ladies were eventually given greater responsibility for vetting candidates for admission from 1940 onwards.

It was decided in 1928 that the girls should be examined medically once a year and dentally every six months but the absence of any regular dental inspection between 1929 and 1935 suggests that Matron and the Ladies' Committee failed to pay heed to dental health in the School. Not surprisingly a considerable amount of dental treatment was required when inspections were resumed.

The Ladies drew fine distinctions on some dietary matters ruling that butter and jam was an extravagant combination on bread. Bread with jam was considered to be unpalatable but bread with margarine and jam was acceptable. In another example of the conditions experienced by the girls a Visitor noted that blankets were thin and the dormitories were cold.

The Schools came under closer Government regulation under the inspection provisions of the Children's Act 1933 which applied to Homes supported wholly or partly by voluntary contributions. Such institutions were required to submit prescribed particulars to the Secretary of State under Part V Section 93 of the Act.

The organisation of annual Garden Fetes and Sales of Work was undertaken by members of the Ladies Committee, in conjunction with Matron, partly to defray the cost of the annual holidays of the girls which were usually taken at Filey. The length of the seaside holiday was doubled to one month in 1935 as a result of an especially successful Garden Fete which raised £35.

From the early 1930s onwards many of the entrants were motherless girls nominated for the School by their fathers, some of whom were required to contribute to the maintenance of their daughters, typically at the rate of 2s.6d per week.

The school was reported to be full in 1936 but, in contrast, no applications for admission were received in 1937. Following operating losses in the Schools of about £1,700 in both 1938 and 1939 proposals were aired for an amalgamation of the boys' and girls' schools and for acceptance of only the neediest children. The Monkgate site could then be sold. These measures were opposed by the Ladies on the grounds they would not be in the best interests of the girls.

The Silver Jubilee was marked with a tea party and river trip to Naburn. Similar treats were provided again two years later to mark the Coronation of King George VI. The celebratory activities organised for the girls on both occasions were on a much smaller scale than for the boys at the Blue Coat school, reflecting the different personalities of the heads of the two institutions.

Little building work was carried out at Monkgate between the Wars but the sick room was re-modelled in 1933 and the sanatorium was completely renovated in 1935 with funds left in memory of Lucy Ross.

At the outbreak of War in September 1939 the basement at Monkgate became a post for Air Raid Wardens and in the following year the air raid shelter for the girls was reinforced. The Ladies agreed to take the girls and staff into their own homes as a temporary measure if the school was rendered uninhabitable by enemy air raids. Some variety in the diet was provided by food parcels presented to the School by the American Red Cross. The older children helped with the washing up once a week at a municipal Civic Restaurant and the girls knitted hundreds of garments for members of H.M. Forces including sixty caps to wear under steel helmets. School was closed on the day after an air raid on York in April 1942.

Few published details are available of the affairs of the School during the war years but the flavour of the period is caught in an account of school life at the time by Dorothy Murfitt (now Mrs Dorothy Brown) who entered the the School with her twin sister Margaret on 12th June 1942. They were eight years old.

On arrival the girls were kitted out with clothes marked with their initials and with toilet requirements. Three pairs of already worn shoes were provided, one for work and play, one for school and one for best.

A washing machine and electric irons were installed in 1948. Until then all washing was done by hand, resulting in very sore fingers. The younger girls laundered on Saturdays and the remainder of the washing was completed on Monday mornings by older girls whose schooling had ended. A fire copper provided supplies of hot water and was also used for boiling clothes. Other laundry equipment including a posser for agitating the clothes in a dolly tub and a scrubbing board. All whites were dolly blued and washed clothes were either ironed with heavy flat irons or passed through a large wooden mangle.

The day began for all children at 6.30 a.m. on weekdays. Each girl had a job to do such as scrubbing floors, whitening the front steps, polishing and dusting, washing up, cleaning cutlery, blackleading grates or rubbing down fenders with emery paper. The children cleaned their own shoes and made their beds. The School baked its own bread until the advent of bread rationing under war conditions.

On Sundays the girls rose half an hour later and were not required to make their beds. They attended church service at 10.30 a.m. and those girls who had been confirmed attended communion once a month. After dinner the girls sat in age order and recited the collect for the day. Successful reciters qualified for their wartime weekly ration of two ounces of confectionery, usually Fry's Cream Tablet or a bar of toffee. Unsuccessful participants had a further opportunity to qualify for their sweet ration during the following week. Later in the afternoon the girls were taken for a walk two by two in a 'crocodile'.

Girl Guides paraded on Wednesday evenings and choir practice took place on Thursday evenings under the direction of a choirmaster, Mr Fryer, who had taught at York Minster. Friday nights were reserved for hair washing and linen changing. A slipper was applied to girls who were caught talking.

Monday evening was set aside for mending underclothes and socks. On the same evening the girls knitted vests in oily wool and were taught to knit their own long and short socks in grey wool. On other weekday evenings the girls were allowed to read or take part in quiet pastimes.

Bedtime was staggered from 6.30 p.m. for the youngest girls to 7.45 p.m. for the oldest who were still at school. Girls between 14 and 16 years of age, who no longer attended lessons and undertook much of the domestic work in the School, were allowed to stay up until 9 p.m. No talking was allowed in bed, but one girl, Eileen, acted as a story teller after the staff had departed. Goblins in the attic made frequent appearances in these tales.

On Saturday afternoons in the summer the girls played rounders or cricket and in the fruit season sometimes scrumped apples from the trees in the garden. The apples would then be secretly consumed in the dormitory at bedtime and cores pushed down a hole in the floorboards under the linoleum.

After the closure of the Blue Coat School the older children attended Burton Stone Lane Secondary Modern School where they were able to mix with other girls and enjoy cookery lessons and a wide range of sports including swimming.

During the wartime years the Annual Service was held at St Michael-le-Belfrey Church on the nearest Wednesday to June 18th with both the Grey Coat girls and Blue Coat boys walking there in traditional costume in a crocodile. 'Jesu joy of man's desiring' was sung as an anthem. After the service the children processed to the Mansion House where prizes and gifts of an orange and a sixpence were distributed by the Lord Mayor and Lady Mayoress.

In the immediate post-war years the girls enjoyed a two week summer holiday at Filey where Matron operated a more relaxed routine. For those girls who stayed at the School for the remainder of the summer holidays occasional outings were organised to the cinema.

The older girls decorated a tree at Christmas and a party was held in January after all the children had returned from their seasonal holiday. The girls received small gifts such as books, games, and colouring books – and also dentifrice toothpaste which was a luxury compared with the standard supply of camphorated chalk.

On leaving school, at 16 years of age, the girls were placed in service and supplied with a set of clothes and a suitcase. The cost of the latter was deducted from their wages.

CHAPTER VIII
The Grey Coat School 1945-1983
A merger and a change of emphasis

THE SCHOOLING OF THE GIRLS came under discussion in November 1945 when the options open to the Schools under proposed new legislation were put to a joint meeting with representatives of the local Education authority. Amongst the alternatives were primary, secondary or boarding School status. The retention of a one-stream grant-aided school depended on recognition by the Ministry of Education and the final option of sending the children to local authority schools was at the discretion of the Executive Committee of the two Charity Schools. In April 1946 the vice-chairman of the Executive Committee, Councillor A.S. Rymer suggested that the purposes for which the Schools had been founded 240 years previously had lost their relevance. He proposed winding up the schools over a period of about two years time and putting the realised assets into a trust to give grants to suitable children to assist with their education – a proposal which was finally adopted some 30 years later.

When it was decided by the Governors to close down the co-educational facilities for the two Schools at St Anthony's Hall at the end of 1946 discussions were held concerning the future of the Girls' School. After an initial consideration of the schooling facilities for the girls it was decided to hand over £1000 of the proceeds of realised investments to the Ladies Committees for them to run a girls' school. This proposal was not proceeded with and instead the girls attended elementary schools in the City from the beginning of 1947.

Agreement was reached to run the Grey Coat School as a girls' hostel for a trial period, under the direction of the Ladies' Committee – which reported periodically to the Gentlemen. The Ladies were allocated half the income of the Charity from investments, together with income from subscriptions, and maintenance payments by parents and guardians of the children in residence.

Three years later it was reported that the maintenance cost per child at Monkgate was 35 shillings per week compared with £3 in local authority institutions. In an accompanying minute, in which Miss Bazzard was thanked for her continued good service, it was confirmed that the big sleeping room at the School would be divided to give some privacy to the senior girls.

The numbers of girls in the School continued to fall slowly and there were deficiencies in the running expenses of the School of £225 in 1951, £388 in 1952 and £819 in 1953. Despite this adverse situation, it was decided, on the advice of the Chairman, Alderman Thompson, that in was in the interest of York ratepayers that the School should continue in existence as it was more economical to run than similar local authority institutions. In a break with tradition in 1953 the Annual Service was held in the Merchant Adventurers' chapel and the Civic Party did not attend. This Coronation year was probably memorable for the girls because they received commemorative spoons and because they had recently been provided with bedside chairs and mats.

The children continued to receive gifts and hospitality from a wide range of organisations in the early 1950s including Royal Air Force units at Full Sutton, Rufforth and Acaster Malbis, the fire service and York 41 Club. By 1954, when there were 19 children in the School, the average maintenance cost per child was £3.10s. a figure which had doubled in three years. A deficit on running expenses of £372 in 1954 raised fresh doubts about the continued future of the School but, after capitalisation of legacies, it emerged that there had been a net increase in capital over the past 7 years of £1100. It became clear that funding was no longer a problem for the School. Indeed it was noted in the minutes of the Ladies' Committee that the capital funds of the School were sufficient to offset the current level of shortfall, namely £800 per annum, for fifty years. The financial affairs of the School were further improved in 1958 when additional income of £600 per annum was provided from the Reginald Hunt Trust.

At a meeting of representatives of local orphanages and homes in 1954 it was confirmed that there was a general shortage of children coming forward for such institutions. Spare capacity was available at Monkgate and it was decided in 1955 to admit boys between the ages of 5 and 9 years. With resident numbers continuing at a depressed level it was suggested in the following year that the placing of an appropriate notification in the *Church Times* might bring forth additional children for the School.

Later in the same year, at a meeting called to discuss the future of the School, serious doubts were expressed regarding the continued need for the type of 'Home' provided by the School in the light of adverse Home Office views about such large institutions. It was decided to examine the merits of building two or three small units on the school cricket field at Stockton Lane by holding discussions with Home Office and local authority representatives and by visiting similar units elsewhere. In the meantime the rundown of the School facilities began with the leasing of part of the cricket field to Heworth Cricket Club. Although the property of the Blue Coat School this field had been used by the girls.

The long term future of the School began to look endangered soon afterwards when a representative from the Home Office explained the implications of the new Children's Act to the Ladies' Committee whereby local authorities now had a responsibility to have a care for every deprived child. It was the personal opinion of the Home Office representative that the existing Grey Coat School premises were no longer suitable and that a smaller and more homely building was more appropriate for the School. The Home Office now favoured boys and girls being brought up together as this approximated more closely to a home environment whilst at the same time giving the boys a sense of security, and of being loved and wanted.

The Civic Party did not attend the Annual Service in 1954 and in 1956 this Service was transferred from St Michael-le-Belfrey to St Helen's Church. In view of the strong ties between the School and the Girls' Friendly Society it was proposed that members of this Society should attend the Annual Service. It was decided that the children would only wear their traditional costumes if the Lord Mayor attended the service. Otherwise they would wear their normal outdoor clothes. Soon afterwards the wearing of uniforms was discontinued altogether because it was felt to be hard on the children, especially the older girls, to be labelled in this way as 'Charity Children'.

Fifteen examples of the traditional uniforms were given to the Castle Museum and, although in poor condition, were worn at an annual Carol Service in the Museum. Some of these sets are still held in the museum. The remaining seventeen outfits were stored at Burton Stone Lane School. It was minuted that other copies of the uniforms had probably been given to the Victoria and Albert Costumes Museum and to Doncaster Museum and Art Gallery.

The Ladies decided to revive the Visitor system in 1956 and invited representatives from 12 organisations in York each to provide a visitor for one month in the year.

Walter Galtress became secretary and treasurer of the School in 1956 and gave faithful service to the Charity for more than 20 years. He had left the Blue Coat School to start his working life at the Station Hotel in 1909. Many years afterwards he became a churchwarden at St Helen's Church where a stained glass window commemorates the link between the Charity Schools and the Church which was the venue latterly of the Annual service.

At the turn of the year it was decided to take short term children into the school because St Stephen's Home was full. There were three instances in the school of girls and small boys from the same family. Miss Bazzard refused to accept a Roman Catholic family because of a Rule that all the girls should attend an Anglican church.

In the following March Miss Bazzard died after 38 years of sterling and conscientious service to the School. She was thought by many to be very straight-laced and was consequently not always popular with the girls. Her contribution latterly was impaired by ill-health but she brought stability and continuity to the institution with consequent benefits for the children. Her regime was summed up by one old pupil as 'prayers and cleanliness'. She left the bulk of her modest estate to the School.

The death of Miss Bazzard was followed by a difficult interregnum including the resignation of the assistant matron and the early departure of the replacement matron on health grounds. This unstable situation was attributed partly to the fact that most of the children entering the School came from broken homes. Four boys proved particularly troublesome before their eventual transfer elsewhere.

The situation in the School was eased in 1959 when an Old Boy of the Bluecoat School, Mr E. Webster, together with his wife, agreed to take over responsibility for the Home until new members of staff took up their posts. Mr Webster also took charge of the children at the annual holiday at Filey, with the four older boys excluded from participation. He was formally elected a Governor soon afterwards. The incoming matron was Miss Jean Bradley, aged 26, who had recently completed a Home Office approved course in child care.

Following the resignation of the some of the older Governors in 1959 in favour of younger members it was agreed that the Ladies' Committee should be strengthened by the co-option of a few male members who would not necessarily be expected to attend every monthly meeting but would agree to take an active part in the running of the Home. The Ladies Committee, together with not more than three men, now formed a General Committee.

In March 1960 another meeting was called to consider the future of the School having regard to modern needs, the smaller numbers of children requiring care and attention, and the fact that local authorities had facilities for almost all children in need of care.

The Governors revived an earlier project, based on Home Office recommendations, for a new custom built Home to accommodate 12 children who were to be distributed between two 'family' units, each looked after by a house mother. Mr A. Mennim, a local architect, was invited to draw up proposals for a pair of houses on the 3.7 acre site of the cricket field at Stockton Lane which eventually became 7 and 9 Stray Garth. The linked units could readily be converted to two semi-detached houses if necessary in the future.

The contract for the two premises was awarded to William Birch & Son at £9,395 and completed two weeks ahead of schedule. New furniture was purchased at a cost of £920. The premises were occupied in mid-April 1961 when the cost of maintaining each child was £6 per week.

In the meantime York Corporation Health Department had offered £17,000, plus fees, for the Monkgate site. This provided a final favourable balance of £5,000 when the move to Stockton Lane was completed. The Monkgate site subsequently became a base for school and dental clinics.

The new premises were opened on the 22nd of June 1962 by Mrs Jean Coggan, wife of the Archbishop designate, in the presence of the Civic party and almost 100 subscribers and friends. Stray Garth was intended to provide security, family love and a chance in life for its occupants. It was generally agreed that the units, with their compact layout and close contact with staff, provided a much more home-like atmosphere, hence the description of a 'Home' rather than a Grey Coat School. In a break with a long tradition the summer holiday of the Home was taken at Bridlington instead of Filey and in 1964 it was transferred to a boarding house at Scarborough.

The numbers of subscribers in 1961, including some commercial firms, had fallen to 26. The total subscriptions amounted to £37, a clear indication that the Home could no longer rely on this particular form of support. Donations and bequests produced £1189 and the deficit for the year was £818.

Two years later Councillor William Thompson, an old Blue Coat scholar resigned after some 30 years of service to the Schools, latterly as Chairman of the Governors, and was succeeded in that office by Councillor J.P. Birch who first joined the Committee in January 1959.

A long-standing matter of concern for the administrators of the Home, reflecting the views of Catherine Cappe some 180 years previously, was the maintenance of school leavers until they were financially self-supporting. This concern had in earlier years led to resident domestic service being favoured as a vocation which eliminated the problem despite the wishes of some girls to pursue other trades or professions. In a measure designed to foster alternative careers for departing scholars, approval was given in principle in 1963 to provide some assistance towards the maintenance of girls between school-leaving age and their 18th birthdays. The Governors resolved legal problems linked with the application of trust funds and agreed to make a weekly ex gratia payment of £1 each to the Cappe Trust for two Grey Coat girls to reside at the Cappe Home at Rawcliffe Holt.

The Home lost a good friend in 1965 with the death of Mr H.E. Harrowell, a York solicitor who was its first President. He had given wise counsel to the charity for a long period of years and had persuaded many people to give substantial financial support to the Home. Mrs Harrowell, who died in 1972, served as a valued member of the Ladies' Committee for over 50 years.

Mrs A.M. Bloor was appointed the new President. Her advancement to such an eminent role in the affairs of the Home did not however encourage her fellow governors to elect all members of the Ladies' Committee as Governors, the title now given to members of the earlier Gentlemens' Committee. The Ladies were invited instead to assemble with the Governors at joint quarterly meetings.

By 1966 the original idea of running two adjacent units at Stray Garth was abandoned and the charity began to operate as a single unit. Proposed structural alterations to facilitate this arrangement were not proceeded with.

Miss Wilson, the House Mother, decided that the summer holiday in 1966 should again be spent at Scarborough. In the following years a variety of holidays were organised including three weeks at Filey in 1968, a stay in a luxury caravan at the coast in 1971 and a visit by 14 children and staff to Butlins at Filey for a week in 1972. A larger party of 16 travelled to Rhos-on-Sea in 1975 and farmhouse holidays were organised in Wales in 1979 and 1980. Two boys attended a Scout camp at Easter in 1972 and two other boys participated in a riding holiday at Pateley Bridge.

Two bicycles were purchased for the boys and another two for the girls. Sally, the dog, was a popular pet and the Home was presented with a cockatiel bird and a tank of fish.

Six children from one family were admitted to the Home in 1967 to be joined soon afterwards by the child of a mother held in Askham Bryan prison. In the following year two mongol babies were admitted and Dr John Newcombe, a consultant in subnormality, briefed members of the Ladies' Committee on the problems and possibilities of looking after such children.

Until 1967 the majority of the children were placed with the Home by the North Riding County Council but, from April of that year, the vacant beds in the Home were taken up by six children from Hull and four from the West Riding. An additional benefit arising from this increase in numbers was the revived success, in October 1967, of the Annual Service and subsequent presentation of gifts to the children by the Lord Mayor and Lady Mayoress. After the 270th Anniversary Service in 1975 the children, staff and members of the Ladies' Committee were entertained at the Mansion House by the Lord Mayor, Councillor J.P. Birch, who was also shortly to become the Chairman of the Children's Trust. In accordance with custom the Lord Mayor and Lady Mayoress gave the children gifts of fruit and money.

The sudden uplift in numbers at Stray Garth rendered inappropriate a proposal to open exploratory talks with a view to a merger with St Stephen's Home. It was agreed however to send two representatives to the quarterly meetings of St Stephen's and vice versa. The surge in numbers was reversed two years later when five children out of a family of six left the Garth.

Early in 1969 the York Childrens' Officer was informed that the Home was prepared to take in children on a short term basis and, in order to extend the catchment area of the unit, representatives from other authorities were invited to inspect the facilities provided. It was agreed subsequently to write to local authorities offering accommodation where problems were being experienced in keeping children of one family together.

A preliminary meeting was held in April 1969 with representatives from St Stephen's Home which was experiencing staffing difficulties. Agreement was soon reached on a merger between the two institutions in a manner which would safeguard the considerable support enjoyed by St Stephen's and retain the goodwill of its friends. A Home Office representative present at the meeting confirmed that there did not appear to be a need for two voluntary homes in York.

In the following month, when a 19 strong joint sub-committee met to resolve details of the amalgamation of St Stephen's Home and the Grey Coat Home, it was decided to discontinue the use of the premises on the Mount, but a proposal to dispose of the house at Filey was not pursued. The existing staff at Stray Garth was judged to be adequate to deal with the proposed combined total number of places for 12 children and one baby. The gardener/handyman at The Mount was to be employed for one or two half days a week at Stray Garth and the Grey Coat Home was accorded first refusal of equipment and other items from St Stephen's. It was also agreed that the combined charities should follow a policy of remaining independent under the terms of the Children and Young Persons Act 1969.

Practical difficulties arose in advancing the scheme because the Charity Schools were registered with the Ministry of Education and St Stephen's was under the jurisdiction of the Charity Commissioners. It was decided that as the Homes were no longer educational establishments they should be registered with the Charity Commissioners.

The advice given by senior representatives of the Home Office in July 1970, on the position of the merged institutions under the Children and Young Persons Act 1969, was that local authorities now possessed sufficient facilities of the type provided by the Home, which could not expect to continue as an Independent Voluntary Body unless it was prepared to specialise. If a suitable form of specialisation could be identified the Home could expect the cooperation of the Yorkshire Regional Planning Committee on Child Care.

By early 1972 the number of children in the Home had fallen to 7 and assurance was sought, and received, from representatives of the local authority that the Home should continue in operation for the time being.

Local organisations continued to give their support to the Home, and the staff at the Retreat provided £100 from the proceeds of their Annual Fete to enable a television set to be purchased. The children were entertained in the Assembly Rooms at Christmas in 1977 by staff from the York Telephone Exchange. Members of the University of York Staff Social Club took the children to the pantomime at York Theatre Royal in the following month.

Miss Wilson, the House Mother left the Home to take up another post in 1972 and was replaced by Miss Ann Shanks. The latter was succeeded by Miss Claire Stableford in October 1974.

A legacy from an Old Boy of the Blue Coat School, W.A. Taylor, was used to purchase a deep freezer for Stray Garth in 1974. Some years later a medal awarded to Mr Taylor was mounted and presented to the Home.

A gift of £500 in 1976 from a group of Girl Guides from the Army on the Rhine was used to purchase a caravan sited on a farm at Warthill. The Guides also donated a colour television set.

The final stage in the life of the previously-named Charity Schools began on 15th February 1973 when, at a meeting of the Grey Coat and Stray Garth sub-committee, it was agreed that Stray Garth was a valuable site and that it was perhaps wrong to have so much money tied up in providing a home for so few children. Rather than moving to a smaller house the Committee favoured using the income of the Charity to help other institutional schemes or individuals on a wide basis. The existing children would be the first charge on the new Trustees. It was agreed to put forward to the Charity Commissioners a series of proposals, drawn up by Mrs Daphne Hey, previously the Honorary Secretary of the St Stephen's Committee. These proposals included a clause that the area covered should be primarily North Yorkshire and Humberside with discretion to cover a wider area. Another clause stipulated that trustees should retire at 75 years of age. In reply the Charity Commissioners set out their requirements:

1. The governing body to consist of 16 trustees with 12 to be named in the original scheme. The trustees should meet quarterly.
2. The governing body to appoint a management committee of 8 people to serve for one year. The members of this committee to be re-appointed annually at the annual general meeting with power to coopt.

3. A house committee of 10 members to administer Stray Garth as long as it shall exist.
4. One third of the Governing Body to be members of the Church of England but no restriction as to creed or religion to be placed on beneficiaries.
5. The benefit of the amalgamated charities to be applied for children and young persons up to the age of 25.
6. No limitations to be placed on the beneficial area.

The object of the proposed York Children's Trust was declared to be the relief of needy children and needy young people under 25 years of age, including the advancement of the education of such children and young persons.

The inaugural meeting of York Children's Trust was held at the Mansion House on the 30th April 1976 after 5 years of legal representation and negotiation by two York solicitors, Mr K.W.H. Bloor and Mr John Shannon. Mr J.P. Birch was elected Chairman of the Trust with Mrs M.E. Wilkinson (the last Chairman of the Ladies' Committee of the Grey Coat School) as Vice Chairman.

As part of the winding down process a valuation of £25,000 was obtained for the Stray Garth buildings with a further sum of £5,000 for the contents. In another move it was agreed that the records of the Schools and Homes should be lodged in the Borthwick Institute.

The funds of St Stephen's Home, the Blue Coat School, the Grey Coat School, the William Richard Beckwith Fund, the Arthur Gill charity, the Matthew Rymer charity and the Ethel Crombie Memorial Fund were all transferred to the Trust.

Meanwhile, following a large increase in staff salaries, it was calculated that the cost of keeping each of the six children aged between 10 and 17 years of age at the Home, of whom half were from the same family, was £16 per week – of which £15 was recovered from the appropriate local authority.

The number of children in the Home fell to four in 1979 and in the following year it was decided to discontinue the Annual Anniversary Service on the grounds that the event was something of an anachronism and probably embarrassing for the older children. Soon afterwards the numbers in residence increased temporarily to nine with the arrival of four children from St Hilda's Home which was closing.

A small increase in numbers at the Home occurred in 1981 when seven schoolchildren and one other girl were in residence. They were cared for by two full-time residential staff, one full-time non-resident staff member and three part-time employees.

The Trust received a legacy of £6,821 from the estate of Miss Bertha Selby in 1982. Part of this sum was allocated to the improvement of the kitchen area at Stray Garth.

In the late 1970s and early 1980s several girls and boys continued to reside at the Home until they reached employment age. Some continued to return to the Home when they had accommodation or other problems. This group of adolescents presented the House Mother – and the Ladies' Committee – with persistent disciplinary problems which were aggravated by the behaviour of some of the younger boys in the Home who were described as lively, rowdy and almost beyond control.

Peter Ferrey succeeded Walter Galtress as Secretary and Treasurer of Stray Garth in 1981 and served the Home and the Children's Trust until his death in 1985 when Mr H.G. Sherriff was appointed Clerk to the Trustees. The Chairman of the Trust, Mr J.P. Birch, acknowledged the value of the work of Mr Ferrey for the two bodies. Subsequently Mr Birch also paid tribute to the very important contribution of Mrs Daphne Hey as the last Honorary Secretary of the Ladies' Committee and also as a member of the Children's Trust.

The Social Services Department of the County Council, which had taken over responsibility for the Home under Local Government reorganisation in 1973, advised against further capital schemes at Stray Garth in 1977 on the grounds that there was an increasing trend, possibly only a temporary phase, away from residential care. The Home received a favourable inspection report from the Department in 1981 together with an assessment that it seemed likely that the Home would be retained for the foreseeable future. This situation was short-lived for, in 1983, it was decided by the Department, under a change of policy, that fostering was preferable to placing children in Homes. Thereafter only disturbed children would be placed in Homes. Four children's Homes in the York area, accommodating a total of 42 children, had already been closed down by the Social Services Department in 1981.

By this time the number of children at Stray Garth had fallen to five, and – in the light of the policy change in favour of fostering – Trust Committee members concluded that the Home had become an unjustifiable drain on the resources of the Trust. The Home closed at the end of October 1983 when four children were transferred to foster homes and the fifth child moved to The Elms Children's Home. It was re-iterated that the Children's Trust would maintain a continuing responsibility for the recent residents of the Home.

At one of their last meetings the members of the Ladies' Committee expressed their warm appreciation of the very long and selfless service performed by their Chairman, Mrs M.E. Wilkinson, and of the tremendous amount of time and trouble she had devoted to the welfare of the children in their care.

Miss Claire Stableford resigned from her post as House Mother a few months before the closure of the Home in order to attend a two year course in Social Work at Manchester University. The Ladies' Committee recorded that her departure would be greatly regretted. She was subsequently sent a piece of furniture from the Home which had been carved by Robert Thompson of Kilburn – the 'Mouseman'.

The Stray Garth premises were sold in 1987 to the Yorkshire Regional Health Authority and occupied by psychiatric patients as part of the community care programme.

So ended a notable institution of the City of York which had provided direct care for children for 278 years. Over the long period from 1705 to 1983 several thousand boys and girls were given the opportunity of an improved start in life and York gained a significant number of useful, and in some cases notable, citizens, including at least two Lord Mayors. The many benefactors gained the satisfaction of knowing that their contributions in time, goods and money had been directed to a very worthy cause.

Finally, thanks to the continuing interest of successive Civic Heads, both residents and visitors received an opportunity, once a year, to enjoy a glimpse in Stonegate or St Helen's Square of one of the long-standing ceremonies and traditions of the City.

C. ST STEPHEN'S HOME 1870-1969

CHAPTER IX

1870-1919
A worthy private charity is born

ST STEPHEN'S HOME WAS FOUNDED, as St Stephen's Orphanage, in Precentor's Court, York in about 1870 to meet the needs of poor orphan children who might otherwise, in the absence of suitable provision in the City, be left destitute. St Stephen was one of the seven deacons charged collectively by the apostles with responsibility for ministering to widows, orphans and the poor.

This private institution was initiated by a group which included Mrs Duncombe, wife of the Dean of York, and her two daughters Mrs Harcourt and Mrs Egerton, together with the Rev. James Douglas, curate at Kirby Misperton. The original building, which was eventually taken down to make way for the Purey Cust Nursing Home, included a small chapel with an altar table and a stained glass window. In its early days the Home provided accommodation for 13 children under the supervision of Miss Mathew and Mrs Blencowe.

The accommodation in Precentor's Court was soon found to be inadequate so by 1872 the orphanage had moved to two houses in Trinity Lane, off Micklegate, where it was run by the same two superintendents, one of whom was described as having a face like a Madonna. Unfortunately the saintly mien was at variance with reports of deception, excessive eating and drinking, and unbecoming conduct in the evenings.

One of the two-storey stucco-rendered houses had lately been in the occupation of Miss Newton. The other house was at one time occupied by a Friends' Boarding School for Girls, the forerunner of the Mount School, which was opened on January 1st 1785 by William and Esther Tuke who lived on the premises until the school moved to Castlegate. The site may have been occupied previously by a soap factory.

An annual payment of up to £9 was specified for each girl but payments on this full scale were only received for three out of seven children. Urgent cases from the York area could be admitted for an entrance fee of £5. Entrants, between the ages of three and ten years, were required to bring with them a full outfit of clothing including one pair of strong boots and six Holland pinafores. Girls had to stay at the Home until after their confirmation.

The financial affairs of the institution were not well managed and the future of the home was in doubt by 1874, when debts of £325 had been accumulated. At that time further expenditure was incurred in altering the Trinity Lane premises, and in buying additional furniture, to enable the number of girls in residence to be increased from 12 to 26. In spite of the recruitment of extra subscribers and helpers, and the soliciting of gifts of old and new clothing, further assistance was required.

The Home was faced with closure until Major William Cayley Worsley and some of his friends provided temporary loans of £125 to cover the period until a legacy of £660 was approved by the Court of Chancery. In later years Canon Body, one time incumbent of Kirby Misperton, was to claim that he had secured the interest of Major and Mrs Worsley of Hovingham. Thus began the crucial support of the Worsley family with successive members continuing to occupy the Chair of the Management Committee until shortly before the closure of the Home.

The legacy of £660, and others, were used to clear off outstanding debts with the result that the Home was left without a capital fund to provide future income. Part of the institution, based at a cottage and premises in Bishopthorpe, was hived off, with Miss Mathew, one of the original superintendents, placed in charge. This operation at Bishopthorpe was in debt and the creditors of the unit were required to relinquish their claims on Trinity Lane in exchange for the security of the property at Bishopthorpe. The number of orphans had by this time expanded from the initial intake of 13 children but numbers were cut back to 18 residents and it was decreed that no child should be admitted permanently without the sanction of a sub-committee.

The re-constituted orphanage was controlled by a committee of twenty-six people which met for the first time, with the Dean of York in the chair, on February 18th 1875. Future anniversaries and jubilees of the Home were based on this date of re-constitution.

The main committee met annually, the managing sub-committee quarterly. Committee members were asked to seek support for the Home from their friends and five hundred copies of an early annual report were distributed for this purpose in 1876. In the following year three hundred cards were circulated to solicit help for a sale of work. Sizeable mail shots were dispatched from time to time throughout the life of the Home, sometimes with discouraging results.

A temporary superintendent, Miss Arlidge aged 22, was appointed on the recommendation of Major Worsley. The new superintendent was assisted by Mrs Worsley together with the Misses Duncombe and Mann, the latter a voluntary worker who took charge of the schoolroom. Miss Arlidge continued to superintend the orphanage until her death 34 years later and received much of the credit for the re-founding and continuing success of the institution throughout the Edwardian era.

Fund raising was a problem from the outset and bazaars organised by influential and distinguished ladies were held in most years. The first of these, a three day event in the Guildhall in 1877, raised the rarely equalled sum of £815. For the first time the Committee had surplus funds and an investment of £500 was made in North Eastern Railway 4% preferred stock.

Major Worsley drew upon a very wide circle of friends and acquaintances to open Sales of Work and other functions connected with the Home. In 1888 a sale at the Home was attended by H.R.H Prince Albert Victor, eldest son of the Prince of Wales and heir presumptive to the throne, who was stationed with his regiment in York.

The premises in Trinity Lane were by now too small to contain the growing family of the home, so the Committee purchased 25 Trinity Lane, a property once owned by the Earl of Shrewsbury. These premises were put into good repair at a cost of £60. The newly acquired buildings provided space for a schoolroom, bathroom and larger dormitories together with a playground which contributed to the health and pleasure of the children. In the following year the adjacent house, 27 Trinity Lane, was purchased and donated by a friend of the institution to provide an additional dining room and a well-ventilated isolation dormitory.

Major Worsley inherited the baronetcy from his father in 1879 and took over the chair of the committee of management of the Home on the death of Dean Duncombe in the following year.

By 1880 there were 31 children in residence and the demand for places could not be satisfied so an adjacent house was taken over, at a rental of £26 per annum, and places provided for 10 more girls. A special fund was set up, amounting to £153, to cover the cost of altering, repairing and furnishing the extension. This acquisition was brought about by the chairman who himself purchased the property on condition that the committee advanced the sum previously invested in North Eastern Railway stock by way of mortgage. Two years later an adjoining workshop was rented and fitted up as a well-lit and airy schoolroom, the same room being used variously as a meeting room, a venue for sales of work, and a playroom in wet weather. After a few years space was released to provide a more fitting chapel for the Home, and the laundry was enlarged with the help of special donations.

In 1883 eight destitute children were received into the Home without any guarantors for the required maintenance payments. The Lady Superintendent resolved this situation by finding a number of friends each willing to meet the fees of a particular child. With these additions the Home was accommodating 49 children by 1885, of whom about half were on a fee-paying basis.

The introduction in 1881 of a summer holiday for the children in the country at 'Wool Knoll', a property owned by Sir William C. Worsley, brought about a welcome change in the annual routine of the Home and a subsequent improvement in the health of the children. After the death of Sir William in 1897 summer holidays were taken at Scarborough House in Scarborough, donated to St Stephen's three years later by Lady Londesborough. The children were carried by rail at a concessionary single fare to this seaside house for at least one month in the year until the outbreak of war with Germany in 1914.

The Home made its own contribution to the community from 1886 when it began to provide dinners in the winter months for poor children from all parts of York, paid for by specially collected funds. The dinners consisted of a basin of Irish stew and a slice of 'roley' pudding, or rice pudding for infants. Mothers of sick children queued with jugs and basins but most of the food was collected by the youngsters themselves. In the early days 36lbs of meat and 8 to 10 stones of potatoes sufficed for 200 children, the food being prepared by a fourteen year old cook assisted by five small kitchen maids from the Home. The uptake soon increased to between 500 and 600 dinners a week and an iron building was provided by Miss Mills to enable meals to be prepared and distributed efficiently. By 1887 10,255 dinners were being provided annually. The funds of the Home were supplemented during this period by sales, every Saturday evening, of donated second hand clothes to the poor mothers of the neighbourhood.

In another development a School of Church Embroidery was established in 1889, under the supervision of Miss Belfield, as a fund raising activity and as a means of creating interest in such work. This was an extension of the activities of the Home which, from its earliest days, had taken orders for surplices, plain needlework and knitting. After moving to a larger room in 1890, the embroidery school contributed a total of £960 to the income of the Home over the next 21 years.

By 1890 the Committee of Management felt sufficiently confident of the soundness of the finances of the Home to purchase all the occupied properties for £1,850, with the help of a mortgage of £700. Four adjoining cottages, and two further cottages, were purchased in the following year to provide a site for the construction of a dining room which would enable all the children to be fed at one sitting. This was achieved when the children all dined together for the first time, with great rejoicing, on Christmas Day 1892. The complete project included a new scullery, a nursery over the dining room, an extension of the playground, a rear entrance to the premises, and a boundary wall to enclose the whole property. The total cost of the building was £1,055 and money was borrowed to finance the scheme. The mortgages were paid off by the end of 1900 and the remaining debts finally cleared in 1906.

In the latter year the Home became a fully equipped school with the addition of a gymnasium, converted from a joiners' shop under the chapel. The sanitary arrangements were remodelled when an outbreak of diphtheria was attributed to defective drains and additional bathroom accommodation was also provided.

After the latest purchase of properties had been completed a Trust Deed was drawn up in 1902 transferring these acquisitions to five trustees namely Sir William Worsley of Hovingham Hall, Miss Arlidge the Lady Superintendent, Baron Wenlock of Escrick Park, Viscount Halifax of Hickleton, and Sir George Cayley of Brompton. In the deed it was stated that the home was 'originated by private enterprise and supported by voluntary subscriptions for the housing, clothing, educating and training of poor orphan girls who have lost one or both parents and generally to assist and help poor children'.

All trustees, members of committees and holders of offices (honorary or otherwise) were required to be members of the Church of England and a priest of that denomination was appointed as chaplain to superintend the religious training of the children. The Lady Superintendent was assigned general charge and superintendence of the Institution with power to select her fellow workers subject to the approval of the managing committee.

Two separate requests were made to the committee in 1902 – by the Archbishop of York and by a parishioner from Kirk Hammerton – to set up branch homes or houses. This led to some fruitless enquiries being made regarding the feasibility of a scheme for a home out in the country.

In the meantime St Stephen's lost two of its most steadfast, influential and caring supporters with the death of Lady Worsley in 1893 and of Sir William C. Worsley in 1897. The latter was described as a 'devoted chairman and ever generous benefactor and friend'. His nephew and successor to the baronetcy, Sir William H.A. Worsley, agreed to maintain the family connection as

Chairman. Although Sir William marshalled many people to help the Home in various ways, attendances by committee members were sparse. Only two of the eight Committee members attended the Annual General Meeting in 1890 and three in 1900.

Another representative of the Worsley family, Susan Lady Worsley, joined the Committee in 1910. At the Annual General Meeting in that year it was claimed that no child was ever turned away from the Home. It was reported that there were currently 52 children in the Home, 2,000 children having passed through the hands of the institution since its inception.

Later in the same year Miss Mary Arlidge died at the age of 56 after serving the home in an honorary capacity for 34 years by devoting her life to the well-being of poor orphan children. She was described as 'a woman of most marvellous gifts and a most fascinating personal attractiveness. She had any amount of individual character which, however, required to be bravely disciplined if it were to be devoted to God's service and for man's good '. She had gathered round her a band of workers whom she inspired with her own ideals. The Committee erected a tall plain memorial cross of Sicilian marble over her grave in York Cemetery.

Shortly after the death of Miss Arlidge a meeting was called at the Guildhall, with Alderman W.H. Birch in the chair, to bring to the attention of well-wishers the financial situation facing the Home following the loss of the long serving Lady Superintendent. The hitherto low operating costs were partly attributable to the fact that both Miss Arlidge, and the current schoolmistress Miss Mann, gave their services in an honorary capacity. The members of the Committee sought to increase subscriptions by £150 per annum to underwrite the salary of the next Lady Superintendent. It was pointed out during the meeting, which was attended by only 13 supporters, that a subscription of £12 would support one girl in the Home for a year. This figure had increased to £15 by the closing years of the First World War.

Some difficulty was experienced in securing a suitable replacement for Miss Arlidge – although the vacant post was widely advertised none of the 127 applicants was thought to be suitable. The position was re-advertised and Miss Rose Hannah Phillips was the eventual successful applicant.

*Dr W.A. Evelyn,
1860-1935.*

Messrs Barron and Barron audited the accounts of the Home from 1904 confirming an operating surplus for the first time in many years in 1911. The total income of £1088 included £296 from donations, £211 from subscriptions and £134 from a sale of work. Payments for children amounted to £260. Almost exactly half the total expenditure of £840 was accounted for by housekeeping costs. The Committee decided in the same year to open the Annual General Meetings to the public in an attempt to increase support.

The name of Dr Evelyn appeared in the minutes of the committee in 1910 when he agreed to review the fire appliances. This general practitioner played an important part in the management of the Home for the next 22 years including service as the honorary medical officer from about 1920.

In March 1911 Dr Evelyn announced that, as a fund-raising venture for the Home, he proposed to arrange a series of five lectures at St William's College entitled 'Walks through York'. In the event these talks, now entitled 'Walks through Old York' and based on a series delivered by Robert Davies in the 1850s, were delivered in St Mary's Hall, Marygate in November 1911 and raised £104 for the Home. Dr Evelyn gave further series of lectures in 1917, 1919, 1921 and 1923 which raised respectively £115, £166, £104 and £170. These talks were of considerable importance in stimulating the interest of citizens in the history and geography of the ancient City.

Information on the activities of the Home during the first World War is limited because the Committee minutes for the period 1912 to 1917 have apparently not survived. The Home was known to be in in debt to the extent of £142 in early 1918 when forty girls were in residence. Five left the Home in 1917, of whom three entered domestic service and two, who were mentally defective, were transferred to other institutions.

It was initially deemed imprudent to send the girls to the seaside at Scarborough in the war-time year of 1918 but the visit was subsequently re-instated. In a further war-time echo it was concluded that the insubordination of some of the older girls was 'nothing more than an evidence of the times we live in'.

After Miss Alice Turner resigned as lady superintendent in September 1919 an advertisement in periodicals for a successor produced 50 replies. The only short-listed candidate who attended for interview was declared to be unsuitable. Miss Catherine Marshall, a governess with the Stapylton family at Myton-on-Swale, was eventually appointed and was to prove an outstanding success in the position.

Thirty nine girls were in residence at the end of 1919, of whom eight were under 6 years of age. The conduct of the girls immediately prior to the arrival of Miss Marshall was described as unsatisfactory and restless, a state of affairs attributed in part to a complete turnover of the staff of Lady Superintendent, Assistant Lady Superintendent, Children's Matron and Kitchen Matron. Two ringleaders were punished by detention and it was proposed to send a another girl to a reformatory. Fortunately this third girl mended her ways and was awarded a good conduct badge at the annual award ceremony a few months later.

At this time the Committee of Management, now called the Executive Committee, met monthly at noon, immediately following gatherings of the Ladies Advisory Committee. The reading of recent entries in the Punishment Book was a routine item on the agenda of the Executive Committee.

In a break with the original regime church attendance was discontinued on Saturday evenings and the Sunday church attendance was reduced from three to two visits. Singing lessons were discontinued when Miss Middleton retired as singing teacher after 18 years. In the busy summer of 1919 a holiday house was rented at Filey for £20 a year and the idea of a Sports Day was mooted. Preparations were made for an annual sale at the Treasurer's House in the autumn and Mrs Raper took children convalescing from whooping cough in pairs to her farm. The children were given presents, as usual, on St Stephen's Day and girls from the Grey Coat School came to tea during the Christmas celebrations. 20 former pupils attended Old Girls' Day and spent the evening at the orphanage.

CHAPTER X

St Stephen's Home
1919-1945
A new home

AT THE NOVEMBER MEETING OF the Management Committee in 1919 Dr Evelyn reported the collapse of a ceiling and concluded that it was essential that other premises should be found for the Home. In support of this recommendation he stated that the health of the children had undoubtedly deteriorated in recent years and that the premises in Trinity Lane were not well suited to the care of young children. He then proposed that a house for sale at 69 The Mount, on the corner of Scarcroft Road, be investigated as a possible site for the Home. Dr Evelyn and the Honorary Treasurer, W.F.H. Thomson of Becketts Bank, were authorised to act in the purchase of the house. The building was a two storey late Georgian property with deep eaves and spacious grounds.

The site formed a part of the estate of the Earls of Egremont until 1837 and was inherited by the eldest illegitimate son of the third Earl, known as Colonel George Wyndham, who was later raised to the peerage as Lord Leconfield. The property was purchased in 1880 by his land agent, William James Clutton whose son, Frank Clutton, sold the property to St Stephen's.

Within 14 days a special meeting of the Executive Committee was called to hear that the house, recently occupied by a Miss Clutton and also Emma Catherine Marshall, had been bought for £4500 with the Orphanage obtaining special preference in the purchase. Colonel Milner, who was particularly keen to acquire 69 The Mount, subsequently offered Nunthorpe Hall in exchange. This offer was rejected because of the high maintenance costs of

No. 25 Trinity Lane.

No. 69 The Mount (by Alfred Gill).

the Hall and the fear that the orphanage would become institutionalised there.

The cost of converting the new premises was £429 and the move to the new Home began in June 1919. The changeover took a week, the girls in the meantime having been sent away to the holiday home at Filey.

As the Executive Committee now carried a debt of £5,000 it sought ways of increasing revenue. It was calculated that the annual cost of keeping a child was approaching £40 and it was decided to ask ladies who charitably supported individual children to increase their contributions to £35.

In 1921, a year when the Home was in serious financial difficulty, a flag day in York raised £152, with the assistance of 100 sellers, and a similar event in Filey brought in £27. In this connection Dr Evelyn was to claim that he was a member of a committee, namely St Stephen's, which started the first flag day in England. This form of fund raising was not welcomed by the Dean of York who commented that flag days destroyed the spirit of giving – people put a shilling in the box when they should have been writing a cheque!

The number of girls in residence fell to 28 early in 1922 but Ministry of Health recognition was achieved in the same year, a classification which authorised the home to receive children from Boards of Guardians. The Executive Committee hoped that this categorisation would lead to an increase in the number of girls entering the home. However this expectation was not realised and resident numbers remained fairly constant for the next two years. It was agreed subsequently to offer places to York City Council when Corporation homes were full. Four years later requests for places were received from Boards of Guardians at Leeds and South Shields, a development which again did not lead to any significant increase in the number of residents. Occasionally children were now being sent out from the Home for adoption, a measure which further depleted their numbers.

The expenses of running the Home in 1922, at £1620, exceeded the income by £132 and another working loss was suffered in the following year when Lord Grimthorpe offered to cover the deficit. The Feoffees of Holy Trinity continued their annual donations of about £30 and their name was, as with other donors, placed over a bed. A suspended bed-sheet or blanket was positioned in the garden of the Home annually for the next 36 years to receive coins from passing racegoers, a form of fund raising which embarrassed some residents. During one Race Week the slender total of about £2 was collected in this manner. A collection box was also fixed permanently in the outside wall of the Home.

The Peaseholme Laundry in York offered to wash all bed quilts free of charge in 1922 and the Filey Laundry usually washed the children's clothes without payment during the summer holidays.

The trustees of the Ethel Crombie Memorial Fund provided £500 in 1924 towards the purchase price of £550 for a holiday house at 35 West Avenue, Filey; responsibility for maintenance of the house rested with St Stephen's. In the same year York Education Committee paid half the cost of children travelling to the Empire Exhibition at Wembley.

In the following year the Archbishop of York dedicated an enlarged chapel at the Home and the Bishop of Whitby replaced the Bishop of Beverley on the Executive Committee.

Dr Evelyn was elected vice chairman of the Executive Committee in 1926 while Mrs Frank Terry was invited to join the committee in the following year. Another long-term supporter of the Home, Miss Helen Argles, acted as honorary secretary. Dr Evelyn proposed that the Lady Superintendent should report half yearly on the welfare and whereabouts of past residents of the Home as a useful guide to the worth and utility of the orphanage which was described by one clergyman as a 'labour of love with very little labour and a great deal of love'.

Half the Trinity Lane property was sold to the Ideal Laundry in 1927 for £1000. The proceeds of a regular pattern of fund raising events, supplemented by an occasional legacy and donations from the proceeds of military tattoos on the Knavesmire, enabled the debit balance of the Home to be reduced to £735 by the end of 1931. Taking into account some special receipts income for that year exceeded expenditure by £489.

Several support groups were active in the early and middle 1930s including a Kirk Hammerton Committee, 33 'Great Friends', and the 'Friends of the Orphanage'. Another source of help was a Pound Day when 366 lbs. of household goods were collected for the store cupboards of the Home together with £13. In a subsequent year 600 eggs were put down in preservative for winter use. When an Aga cooker was installed the suppliers donated cooking utensils and plate racks. A booklet advertising a Sale of Work and other events was distributed to 10,000 houses in York and a fund collector was employed by the Home on a 10% commission basis. Another fund raising venture was the production of a calendar for sale on behalf of the Home. A broadcast appeal by the BBC in 1934 produced disappointing shared proceeds of £16. These examples indicate the scale and variety of voluntary effort required to produce a modest level of financial support during the unfavourable economic climate in the early 1930s.

The proposed acceptance of a Wesleyan Methodist child from the Ryedale Guardians in 1932 called for an ecumenical compromise in the Home with its Church of England background and links. It was eventually agreed that the eight year old girl could be admitted if she was of satisfactory moral character and could be brought up as a member of the Church of England.

Susan, Lady Worsley died in 1933 after serving the Home generously and devotedly as a member of the Executive and other committees for over 20 years. In the same year Mr Brotherton gave a donation of £100 on the occasion of his marriage to Miss Worsley. He subsequently became a trustee of the Home and agreed to pay for the maintenance of a child. The Home lost another major supporter in 1936 with the death of Sir William Worsley whose 'wisdom, sound judgement and leadership will long be remembered by all whom he worked with and for at the home.' A commemorative Worsley wing was opened at the Home in 1939 and the inscribed plaque remains in situ.

The Worsley wing was intended to be used as a sick bay and sanatorium to supplement the day and night nursery in the Home. In the early 1940s the wing was used as a day nursery for the children of working mothers.

The succeeding Sir William Worsley accepted the invitation of the President, the Archbishop of York, to succeed his father as chairman of the Executive Committee. Lady Joyce Worsley took over the chairmanship when Sir William left for military service in 1939 and was to hold this office for the next 34 years.

Doctor Evelyn died in 1935 after making an outstanding contribution to the running of the Home over a quarter of a century as a leading committee member, fund raiser and medical officer. His family was not in favour of any form of memorial at the Home and asked mourners at his funeral to send donations to the Home instead of providing floral tributes.

The Diamond Jubilee year of the Home in 1935, coinciding with the Silver Jubilee of King George V, was a time of financial crisis for the institution so a sub-committee was formed to investigate the possible disposal of the whole, or part, of the land belonging to the Home for building purposes. The outcome was the sale of the paddock to Messrs Brisby for £1600. Some of this money was used to re-paint the outside of the premises and, by the following year, the financial situation was judged to be satisfactory despite a fall in subscriptions in recent years.

The girls were given two shillings per head as a part of the celebrations of the Coronation of King George VI in 1937, but representatives of the Home were unable to attend a Rally of Youth in London because of an outbreak of sickness. Instead the Home was visited by the Archbishop of York and also by the Duchess of Devonshire. At that time there were 27 girls in residence including a year old baby.

Offers to accommodate Basque refugees in 1938 were not taken up, nor was a similar offer to house two Jewish refugees. In 1940 a Jewish mother was accommodated with her child under an arrangement whereby the mother helped in the Home. Four years later the Home took in a mother and her two children after their home had been destroyed during an air raid on London.

At the time of the Munich crisis in the autumn of 1938 trenches were dug in the garden as an air raid precaution and filled in again two months later. Corrugated iron coverings above the trenches were intended to provide protection against the weather. Sir

Miss Marshall (centre) and her charges.

William Worsley offered a house at Hovingham if evacuation of the Home became necessary.

A successful radio broadcast appeal by Sir William in March 1939 brought in the welcome sum of £227. The appeal was backed up by a publicity photograph in *The Radio Times*, notices in buses, gummed stickers on letters and the circulation of 1500 postcards signed by Sir William. One outcome of the appeal was the formation of a band of supporters drawn from men working on the railway.

The children were evacuated to the home of Mrs Stapylton at Myton-on-Swale on the outbreak of war in September 1939. Their hostess was paid five shillings per week for each child and member of staff. For several months the children enjoyed a different life style in country surroundings where they attended the village school and were able to watch milking, butter churning and shoeing.

Meanwhile the potting shed at the Home was converted into an air raid shelter by strengthening the walls and adding a concrete roof. Bunks were fitted in the shelter and anti-splinter netting applied to the windows. Soon after the completion of the shelter the girls returned from Myton to York. During an air raid on York, when enemy bombs fell on the nearby Bar Convent, the girls sang hymns in the air raid shelter. To relieve the extra burdens on the staff a 65 year old woman was engaged as a fire watcher to douse enemy incendiary bombs. This appointment was short-lived as was the introduction of a three-member 'War-time Executive Committee'. Despite wartime constraints the girls enjoyed a holiday at Filey in July 1940. Shortly afterwards the seaside house was offered to the local military authorities and, in order to leave the premises suitable for army use, the furniture was offered for sale.

Several former residents have supplied some details of life at the school in the early 1940s. One girl described St Stephen's as a real home where she felt secure. Discipline was strict and enforced for minor offences, either with a galosh kept hanging in the staff bathroom, or by the back of a hair brush. Sweets were only given out as special treats but the children traded apples taken from trees in the garden for sweets supplied by their fellow pupils at local schools. The adjacent chip shop provided additional food supplies for girls lucky enough to possess a few coppers.

The infants attended St Clement's school and older girls attended Scarcroft Road, Priory Street, or Mill Mount in the case of girls who had passed scholarship examinations.

The Home uniform included turkey red pinafores and coats with velvet collars. Shoes were kept in a large cupboard and handed down through the Home until they were finally worn out. Each girl was allotted chores to be completed before she went to school including bed making, scrubbing and polishing. The nightly bath – two to a bath for the younger children – was followed by bed time stories read from Beatrix Potter by various readers including Mother Catherine and girls from Mill Mount School.

The day began on Sundays with Communion services taken in the chapel by Canon Hardy accompanied by Miss Marshall on the organ. Morning service followed at St Clement's Church on Scarcroft Road. Sunday afternoons were occupied with learning a Collect or Psalm, except at Easter when the girls searched the grounds for hidden Easter eggs accompanied by Sandy, the dog.

The strong religious atmosphere in the Home was reflected in the naming of rooms after saints.

At Christmas the midnight service was followed by a dormitory feast including mince and pork pies. This was a prelude to St Stephen's Day, or Boxing Day, celebrations – the most important in the annual calendar. A nativity play was staged for Committee members and friends and the children received presents and prizes from the Christmas tree.

A later generation in the early 1950s received three pence a week pocket money for children with surviving parents and double that amount for orphans. The girls were allowed to attend the Saturday morning film show at the Odeon cinema.

Members of the Worsley family took ciné films of the activities at the Home which were shown during the course of an annual visit by the children to Hovingham. The girls were entertained to lunch in private homes followed by tea at the Hall with Sir William and Lady Worsley.

As a war-time measure the normal bazaars, or sales of work, were replaced by 'phantom sales', virtually appeals for donations, which raised almost as much money as full-scale events. Advertising space was taken in local newspapers in an attempt to attract funds, the first entitled 'Please be a Father Christmas to our little ones'. However, because the residents received so many treats in this particular Festive season, the £65 raised by the advertisement was put into a Welfare Account to buy clothes for the children. In another war-time scheme a letter was sent to all local employers asking their employees to contribute a farthing a week to the Home, equivalent to just over a shilling a year. Another offer of help came from a soldier billeted at the Home in the later years of the war who decorated several rooms at his own expense as an expression of gratitude for the kindness he had received there.

In July 1940 the executive committee examined a proposal to evacuate the children to Canada. This project was temporarily halted because there were no places immediately available. Instead Mrs Cooke Yarburgh offered to accommodate four children ineligible for overseas evacuation at her home in Scotland.

After the first World War the numbers of orphans in the Home had gradually declined and in mid-1940 several 'Old Girls' requested a change of name from the unpopular 'Orphanage'. Soon afterwards the simpler title 'St Stephen's' was adopted. In the meantime a few younger boys were admitted and by 1942 there were 23 girls and 3 boys in residence, of whom about a half were temporary residents. The approximate weekly cost per child was twenty four shillings and it was agreed that no temporary children would be admitted for less than twenty five shillings per week.

The future of the Home came under discussion in 1942 and, at a very full meeting in September of that year, the Dean of York gave a report of the work of the Kiltner Sisters with the possibility of the Home becoming an annexe of the Kiltner Sisters' School. Subsequently it was resolved to carry on the Home and to balance the budget by accepting a further four children. By this time the Lady Superintendent, Miss Marshall, – usually known as 'Mother' or 'Sister Catherine' – was over 70 years of age. It was decided that she should be allowed to retire with a supplemented pension and that a younger Matron should be sought. Members of the committee were asked to subscribe an extra £26 per annum between them in order to augment Miss Marshall's pension when she left to live with her sister in Dorking.

The first replacement Matron was not satisfactory and another Matron was appointed. In the meantime the Kitchen Matron and Nursing Sister had left to join the Land Army as farm workers. A small Homes Committee met once a week to assist Matron with the financial affairs and general running of the Home. Preferential consideration for admission was granted where a mother could not herself look after her children. In view of the old-fashioned physical structure of the premises the Ministry of Health Inspector was requested to discontinue visiting the Home as an approved institution. This removal of St Stephen's from the list of Ministry approved homes prompted the resignation of the then Matron who also complained that the house was not suitable for small children and that there was an absence of suitable assistant staff. These staffing problems were linked with complaints that for several months the behaviour of some of the twenty children, of whom three were day boarders, had been poor.

In February 1944 a Ministry of Health representative defined the requirements to be fulfilled if the Home was to be re-instated on the Ministry approved list. The main stipulations were that daily boarding should be discontinued and that the maximum number of children in residence should not exceed 28 – of whom not more than six were to be under five years of age. A small amount of plumbing was required to upgrade facilities, a diet book must be kept, medical cards introduced and routine medical examinations conducted every three months. Bedside mats were called for and towel and face cloths had to be kept separate for each child. Later the Ministry specified further requirements including extensive re-decorating.

During the period when the specified changes were being introduced a visiting Inspector from the Children's Branch of the Home Office suggested that St Stephen's should be turned into a Home Office approved school for girls from 10 to 15 years of age, of whom 50% would have been before the courts. The local committee would remain but the Home Office would appoint a head mistress. The Home could revert to an orphanage on giving one month's notice but, in the opinion of the Home Office, the time for small children's homes was past.

The Executive Committee next sought the views of the Ministry of Health which thought that St Stephen's was doing useful work and that there was a need for the Home in the district. The Ministry of Health said it was interested in keeping open all children's homes where there was a need for them. The Executive Committee accordingly rejected the views of the Home Office inspector and discarded the idea of an approved school. After a further inspection visit in December 1944 the Ministry of Health agreed to issue the necessary certificate of suitability provided that the specified plumbing work was completed satisfactorily. A further condition was that the numbers of resident children should be reduced from 28 to 24, and subsequently to 23. The certificate of suitability under section 54 of the Poor Law Act of 1930 was duly issued in July 1945.

A new matron, Miss Gowan, was appointed in March 1944 and retired after four months on health grounds. She recommended that the then house matron, Sister Cobb, who had been passed over previously as a candidate for the post of matron, was well suited to the job. This proved a happy appointment for Matron Cobb continued successfully in the post for 22 years until she reached retirement age. Miss Gowan subsequently became a valuable member of the Executive Committee. At about this time another successful long-term appointment was that of Mrs Daphne Hey as honorary secretary of the Home. Her clear, very legible and extensive minutes, provide valuable information regarding the activities of the Home.

In 1945 the Committee decided that girls should be deterred from leaving before the age of 16 years. School-leavers were to remain in residence and act as house-girls whilst receiving training in all forms of home and mother craft. They received pocket money of five shillings a week out of which they were encouraged to save one half. No girl was allowed to leave the school without the consent of the executive committee which was required to ascertain whether the girl was continuing her training or accepting a suitable post. In order to extend the social life of the girls the enlightened executive committee thought it would be a good idea for the children to meet suitable boys and invite them home for tea.

CHAPTER XI

St Stephen's Home 1945-1969 A final change of role

FUND RAISING ACTIVITIES WERE increased after the Second World War and included shared flag-days with the Charity Schools. Mr Noel Terry opened his garden at 'Goddards' on Tadcaster Road for the benefit of the Home on several occasions. A broadcast appeal by the Bishop of Selby in April 1948 brought in the handsome sum of £1,258.

The house at Filey was handed back by the army authorities, and let to other charitable organisations including the Grey Coat School. St Stephen's continued to retain occupancy for its own younger girls for two weeks during August while four older girls were allowed to make separate holiday arrangements. At this time the house was poorly equipped and when the girls spent six weeks at the house in the summer of 1950, the property was described as providing what was tantamount to a camping holiday. The house continued to belong to the Ethel Crombie Memorial fund with provision for St Stephen's to maintain the house, sub-let the property and retain any rental income. A sub-committee was appointed in 1952 to review its future and it was decided to retain it and accept an offer of maintenance assistance from Filey Rotarians. Within a year the house had been put in good repair and fitted out with a full complement of furniture. Mrs Richardson, the wife of a local doctor, began to take an interest in the maintenance of the house and its contents, a task which she continued for twenty years. She was elected to the Executive Committee which held one of its regular monthly meetings each year at the house in Filey.

In the early post war years the numbers of residents in the Home were in the 15-20 range and housekeeping costs were 10s. 8d. per head per week. The new matron was credited with a reduction of 7d. a head from the corresponding figure in the previous year. By this time the children had moved for Sunday services to St Clement's from Holy Trinity in Micklegate; the younger girls however remained with the Holy Trinity Brownie pack. In a new venture for the Home five children aged eight to thirteen years were admitted at the request of Leeds Social Welfare Committee, to be followed soon afterwards by two children from the Children's Department of Lancashire County Council. This brought the number of residents up to the permitted maximum of 23. The wide geographical spread of parents contributing towards the upkeep of the children increased the workload of the honorary treasurer in collecting the frequent arrears of payments.

Official responsibility for the Home was transferred from the Ministry of Health to the Children's branch of the Home Office in mid-1948. In his last routine report some months earlier the Ministry of Health Inspector had commented favourably on the happy atmosphere. He also observed that Matron Cobb was too conscientious in that she did not take her holidays or full amount of off-duty time. Despite this favourable report a Visitor nominated by the Executive Committee commented in late 1948 on the dreadful condition of the laundry and lavatories, and thought it might be wiser to move to a more compact and modern house. This latter recommendation was influenced by the high average expenditure of £75 per annum on domestic repairs over the preceding five years.

In 1948 funds were received from a variety of sources including £27 from a sale of an Ayrshire cow at auction, £50 from Escrick Nurses Association when it was taken over by the National Health Service, £200 from the trustees of Sir James Reckitts and £250 from the York County and District Hospital Contributory Scheme. In a separate move to increase revenue the Home joined the National Council of Associated Children's Homes and sought its continuing advice on the rates of maintenance to be charged for children placed by local authorities. The Association held some of its local meetings at St Stephen's.

Disciplinary problems were encountered in 1949 when two cases of alleged maltreatment of children were investigated by a Home Office inspector. An official grant of funds was temporarily withheld and, from then onwards, the smacking of children was restricted to the matron. The children's pocket money, locker facilities and personal toilet equipment were all found to be inadequate by the Inspector.

In the following year a memorandum from the Home Office recommended a medical examination for staff, a record book of events, a punishment book and attendance at child care courses by staff. Home Office policy came to the fore again in 1953 when it was ruled that girls over 15 years of age should move on to hostels. Girls were allowed to continue in residence under the house-girl scheme so long as they were receiving proper training and not merely being used as domestic help. They were to be treated as proper members of staff and, in accordance with a scheme run by Dr Barnardos, to receive pocket money of five shillings a week and a credit allowance for clothes – the latter to be spent under the supervision of Matron. The Home Office agreed that 'when in doubt the Committee should do what a good and wise parent would do in the best interests of the child'.

A review of the distribution of supervisory responsibilities in 1952 confirmed that the House Committee would deal with admissions, scrutinise bills and look after the furniture. The Executive Committee retained responsibility for the premises, for the conduct of the Home, for passing bills for payment and for determining when girls could finally leave the Home. Within a year there were complaints that the House Committee was overloaded with work.

Later the same year the National Spastics Society commenced protracted negotiations for the use of the vacant wing of the Home as a clinic for special children, a facility which was finally brought into use in March 1954.

Ten girls attended Knavesmire School and were kitted out with blue blouses and navy cardigans to wear with their gym tunics. Members of the executive committee investigated why none of these girls moved on to grammar schools and concluded that the St

Stephen's pupils faced too much competition for the 100 places available in the City of York.

The children were widely entertained at the time of the Coronation of Queen Elizabeth and favourable comments were passed on their good behaviour and manners at commemorative parties. They were loaned a television set by Cussins and Light to watch the Crowning of the Queen and were given their own set in the following year. The Home returned some of the hospitality received by making its grounds freely available in the summer months for garden parties arranged by local organisations.

Mrs Willson-Pepper, a long standing member of the Executive Committee, stimulated York Corporation in 1954 to support the provision of a hostel at Rawcliffe Holt where older girls could live cheaply and under supervision. Assistance with the project was received from the Rowntree Village Trust. This was a development of the concept put forward by Catherine Cappe some 150 years earlier so the home was named after her. The project countered criticism from the Home Office that working girls had continued in residence at St Stephen's. Rawcliffe Holt became available for these girls in January 1955. Three years later a cottage which the girls could run themselves was opened in the grounds.

The house at Filey remained in extensive use after additional equipment was purchased and sanitary facilities improved. The Oldham Children's Officer suggested that her department should rent the house for extended periods each summer, an arrangement which continued for several years. The Grey Coat School continued to use the premises, with Dewsbury Children's Department also renting the house in 1956. The Civic Party from Oldham visited the house in 1958 and, after noting that the decorations and amenities left much to be desired, the Mayor agreed to hold a social function with the proceeds earmarked for the Filey house. These Oldham links, and financial contributions, had the effect of keeping the amenities at the Filey house up to scratch and offset the damage to the property and equipment which was attributed to the Oldham tenants. The introduction of an inventory alleviated this problem. Unsuccessful attempts were made over several years, with the assistance of house agents, to find private lettings for the house. Tenants in the early 1960s included both Rochdale and Huddersfield

Church of England Children's Societies, East Suffolk County Council and Ipswich Children's Department.

Fund raising efforts continued to draw upon the energies of Committee members. A broadcast appeal made by Lady Cayley in October 1955 raised £214 for the Home. Two years later 63 people responded to a series of appeal letters. A different form of assistance was provided by a painter from Dodsworths, a local firm, who offered to decorate the premises in his spare time. His employers provided paint and equipment.

The numbers of children fell to 17 by the mid 1950s and a reduction in the total staff of five was proposed. About that time the Home was requested to take in a small boy with his sister. Whereas such boys had left the Home in the past at five years of age Home Office policy now required that they be kept in residence until school leaving age. The committee decided to continue accepting brothers with their sisters and by 1957, there were fourteen girls and ten boys at St Stephen's.

Dr Mungall took up the appointment of medical officer in the mid 1950s. His recommendation to inoculate the children with poliomyelitis vaccine was not accepted by the respective parents. The Home Office suggested that the children be weighed and measured every three months.

Mary O'Loughlin, a St Stephen's girl, was chosen in 1956 from the 300 girls at Knavesmire School to be Head Prefect. In later years, at her wedding which was attended by Matron, she confirmed that she had been very happy at St Stephen's. Several girls and boys became prefects and Girl Guide leaders and June Richmond won a Schools Athletic Cup. In 1962 Ruth Sheriff passed her 11 plus examination and gained a place at Mill Mount School. The other children transferred to the new Knavesmire School in 1964.

At that time the home included a large kitchen with Aga stove and pantry, two sculleries, a large dining room, a sewing room, a sitting room/office, two cloak rooms, the chapel, children's dormitories and bathrooms, together with staff accommodation.

The numbers of children continued to hover around the permitted capacity of 23 and the Executive Committee agreed to provide temporary accommodation for Old Girls who had run into domestic problems. The upkeep of five children was paid for by their parents, sixteen were supported by local authority contributions and two children were accommodated without any financial support. In 1957 the honorary treasurer pointed out that there was only one child who was not in the care of a local authority. He accordingly recommended that appeals to the general public for financial support should be made 'with care'. The Home was now experiencing a high turnover of children with 16 new arrivals and 15 leavers in 1958. Matron, together with the assistant matron, Miss Irene Church, and the support staff coped well with this changing situation and the House Committee decided in 1961 that everything was running so smoothly that monthly meetings were no longer required.

Two years later staff problems kept recurring and an advertisement for a sister, in five newspapers and periodicals, produced only one applicant who then took another job instead. Matron cooked the Christmas dinner single handed because the cook had left; her daughter Margery helped out during some staff crises.

Two items continued to appear in the minutes of the committees – the departure of the cook, usually at short notice, and the need to replace worn-out floor linoleum in one room or another.

Problems were experienced in the early 1960s with backward older children who were bullying the younger ones; the incidence of children running away and staying out overnight increased and some petty crime was encountered. Matron experienced a period of ill-health at a time when she was dealing with three trying older girls who provided a bad example for the other children. Several fires were started deliberately in cupboards and elsewhere over a period of years, incidents which confirmed the wisdom of a Home Office ruling that the children should wear pyjamas made of flame resistant material. As a further fire precaution the rope fire escape at the Filey house was replaced by an expensive rigid version which was paid for out of a legacy.

Several legacies flowed in during the mid-1950s so the domestic equipment was upgraded with the purchase of a washing machine, a refrigerator and a floor polisher. A seesaw and a climbing frame were also acquired and a Mrs Beechey donated a television set she had won at the races. The finances were gradually built up over the post-war years as immediate and deferred legacies continued to flow in. By 1961 the invested funds amounted to £7,000 supplemented by £1,300 in short term accounts. Barron and Barron continued to audit the accounts after 61 years and returned their fee as a subscription. In 1963 a Certificate of Registration under the Charities Act was received as confirmation of the status of the Home.

It is perhaps ironic that for most of its life the Home struggled hard to make ends meet with the help of a wide variety of fund raising schemes which entailed much hard work, sometimes for a very modest return. In its final years legacies flowed from past supporters, some of whom had probably been the recipients of a considerable volume of annual reports and special appeals to stimulate their interest in the Home. Other testators may have heard of the merits of the Home through the Worsley family, through other committee members or from their solicitors.

New donors included the Variety Club of Great Britain, the Lions Club, the staff of RAF Linton upon Ouse and York telephone exchange. The latter subscribed three pence per week from their wages to provide birthday presents, Easter eggs and seaside outings. Parties at the Fire Station were particularly popular because the children were taken home on fire engines. Employees of the Mecca dance hall bought all the children winter coats. Twelve churches sent gifts from their harvest festival, a figure which rose to 32 churches in subsequent years. In its turn St Stephen's continued to provide facilities for garden fetes and other outdoor events for organisations in the neighbourhood.

In a change in style a Coffee Party and Bring and Buy sale at the De Grey Rooms in 1960 was organised without the traditional speeches and opening by a local dignitary. Another new departure was the omission of speakers from the Annual General Meetings which now became what was described as purely formal events. The tradition of giving Christmas gifts to Matron and her staff was retained and, in a thoughtful gesture in 1960, one gift took the form of an air ticket to enable Matron to visit her daughter in Naples in the Spring. In a later year Matron's Christmas gift took the form of a holiday in Spain.

Amongst the tenants of unoccupied parts of the house was Mr Alfred Gill, a well-known local artist. He made a sketch of the Home as the illustration for the front cover of the Annual Report for 1960 in place of the usual photograph for which the block had been lost. Mr Gill renovated the loft at his own expense in return for a 14 year lease. Previous tenants of the loft had included a local joiner and Boy Scouts. A flat on the premises was also available for letting.

Another generation of the Worsley family became interested in the work of the Home when Miss Katharine Worsley helped to care for the children over several years in the 1950s prior to her marriage to H.R.H. the Duke of Kent at York Minster in the summer of 1961. She was known by the girls as Aunty Kathy and is remembered with great affection, particularly for reading bed-time stories. She also scrubbed floors, mended clothes and helped in the nursery. Her mother, Lady Worsley, ended her long and conscientious period of service on the Executive Committee in 1973 when she was presented with the sketch of the house by Alfred Gill. The retirement of Lady Worsley, after 34 years as Committee Chairman, marked the end of the involvement of the Worsley family, an association which had extended over almost 100 years. It is no exaggeration to claim that, without the continuous, dedicated and generous support of the Worsley family, St Stephen's Home would have operated generally on a more restricted scale and would have been faced with closure on a number of occasions.

The steady decline in the average numbers of children, from 22 in 1957 to 14 in 1966, led Matron to express concern at the cost of running a large old house for a decreasing number of occupants. She suggested that a smaller, and more suitable, house should be built in the garden. As part of the long run down of the Home the monthly service in St Stephen's chapel was discontinued in 1967.

Meanwhile at Filey the popularity of the house was increasing and a ship-borne Pirate Radio Station, due to operate off Filey, offered to put out an appeal over the air for St Stephen's. Over the years useful sums of money were collected by tin-rattling in Filey, usually under the auspices of the Rotary Club. A wide range of organisations rented the property from late May through to early September in 1966, including the Hull Sailors' Children's Society, the revenue from which augmented the income of St Stephen's.

In a moving gesture in 1968 a donation was received from the cabin crews of British Overseas Airways Corporation in memory of Barbara Jean Harrison, an Old Girl, who was killed when a Boeing 707 crashed at Heathrow Airport.

The Home Office encouraged staff in voluntary homes to obtain a suitable qualification by agreeing to award a 'Declaration of Recognition of Experience in the Residential Care of Children' to long serving older staff. Matron Cobb had attended a Home Office staff refresher course some 20 years previously and, as she was now approaching retirement age, decided not to apply for this new form of recognition.

The Executive Committee continued its practice of giving Christmas gifts to the staff – as recorded in the committee minutes. Vera, Bessie and Cook, the domestic staff, received gifts of money and vouchers were presented to Mrs Walker and Miss Privett. Mr Sturdy, the gardener, received a supply of cigarettes and a good transistor radio was provided for Matron Cobb. Amongst the many seasonal events organised for the children was a fireworks party in the garden. In the previous year, as an experiment, Matron allowed some of the girls to spend Christmas Day with female staff employed at the York telephone exchange. The seasonal festivities in that year were described in very glowing terms.

Mrs Cobb retired at the end of 1968 and a bungalow was purchased for her in Beech Avenue, Bishopthorpe. Provision had been made for supplementing her pension with the assistance of matured insurance policies and funds set aside.

At a meeting about this time with a Home Office representative and the York Children's Officer the position of St Stephen's was reviewed. It was generally agreed that an Assistant Matron was required to give more help to Matron. It was also confirmed that there continued to be scope for skilled residential work, particularly for homes which could take families of children. Hopes were held out that the forthcoming Regional Planning Boards in Child Care, with representatives from voluntary homes, would provide more generous help for such homes in the future.

It was initially decided that the replacement for Matron Cobb should take the form of a married couple with the husband working outside the Home. Training in child care would be provided for the wife. Instead a Matron was appointed to take up her post when Matron Cobb retired. At this stage there were sometimes only five children in residence.

The new Matron left after a week in post and, as an emergency arrangement in early 1969, the eight children in residence were dispersed, four to their mothers and two to the Grey Coat Home at Stray Garth. Places were reserved at the latter Home for the two remaining girls who were temporarily absent.

Liaison with the Grey Coat Home had became closer in 1968 with an exchange of Committee members. A meeting was arranged in April 1969 with representatives of the Home Office, and the York Children's Department, together with the Committee of the Grey Coat Home, when it emerged that there was no requirement for two voluntary children's homes in York.

It was agreed subsequently to amalgamate St Stephen's and the Grey Coat School but, in order to preserve the goodwill of St Stephen's, care was taken to avoid any suggestion that St Stephen's was closing down. This information was released in a delayed press statement on August 14 1969.

So ended the working life of the Home as a separate institution after almost 100 years of providing a caring home life for orphans in the early days of the venture, and for children with difficult home circumstances latterly.

It was fitting in its final year that one of the children from St Stephen's, Violet Brittain, should win a Duke of Edinburgh's Gold Medal Award which was presented to her at Buckingham Palace.

The dispersal of the property of St Stephen's began with the fish and chip shop, between the Home itself and the Abbey Park Hotel, being sold to the Hotel. The flat was offered to the University of York for use by a member of staff. The Women's Group of the University had been allowed the use of the dining room, playroom, kitchen and cloakroom as a creche on two mornings a week alternating with the successful Scarcroft Play Group. The University group soon progressed to a five day operation and provided lunches for its children. When the University group eventually vacated the premises it was given a rocking horse by the St Stephen's committee. The organ was given to Neil Williams who wished to restore it, and then play it.

The house at Filey was retained for a year and then sold for £2,000, with the spare contents handed over to Girl Guides in Filey. Mrs Richardson, who had dutifully looked after matters connected with the Filey house since its restoration in 1952, resigned from the Executive Committee. The proceeds of the sale of the house reverted to the Ethel Crombie Memorial Trust. The funds of this Trust were in turn merged with the assets of the York Children's Trust along with the funds of a number of other small trusts.

The Home was listed as a building of special architectural and historical interest in 1972. Surprisingly this was soon followed by a proposal that the premises should be demolished under a proposed new ring road scheme which was subsequently abandoned. As a temporary measure the house was used to accommodate a summer school for French Canadian children. In 1975 a further plan was approved for the house to become a dancing school and later in the same year plans were put forward for conversion to a self catering hotel. Finally in 1976 the premises were sold to the Shepherd Group for use as offices.

A strong bond exists between many surviving pupils. Mrs Monica Leak, who lived at St Stephen's for eleven years between 1932 and 1943, organised a reunion at the former Home in 1990. The party was joined by two members of the Auxiliary Territorial Service who had entertained about thirty of the children during the early years of the Second World War.

Epilogue

THE CULMINATION OF THE long story involving the Blue and Grey Coat Schools, St Stephen's Home and several other charities is the formation of the YORK CHILDREN'S TRUST.

The Trust continues to provide vital assistance, not only to children but also to young people under the age of twenty five years.

The York Children's Trust became fully operational on the closure of the Family Group Home at Stray Garth, York in 1983.

According to the Trust Deed 'the object of the York Children's Trust shall be the relief of needy children and needy young people under 25 years of age, including the advancement of the education of such children and young persons'. It is the responsibility of the Trustees to carry out these aims, giving priority to children in York and the surrounding districts.

A large proportion of funds goes for the relief of suffering and sickness. The Trustees appreciate that children may also have needs in a broader cultural or artistic sense. They are, therefore, prepared to consider making grants to young people for projects such as voluntary service overseas, participation in organised expeditions at home and abroad, and occasionally in furtherance of training where official help is not forthcoming.

Finally the Trust is playing an ever widening role in child support and care, and to this end co-operates with various statutory bodies. The Trust has 16 members and the Clerk to the Trust is Mr Bert Sherriff.

JACK P. BIRCH
Chairman

Trustees of the York Children's Trust 1996

Mr J.P. Birch, OBE, JP, *Chairman*
Mrs M.E. Wilkinson, *Vice-Chairman*
Miss L.J. Hill
Mrs A. Hope
Lady M. Fitzalan Howard
Mrs K. Lethem
Mrs E.M. Mungall, JP
Mrs R.J. Wilson
Dr H.J. Heggarty
Mr G. Hierons, JP
Mr R.W. Miers
Mr C.P. Roberts, JP
Mr W.M. Sessions, JP
Mrs A. Smith
Rev G. Webster

Clerk to the Trustees:
Mr Bert Sherriff
23 Muncastergate, York YO3 9JX
Telephone (01904) 423382

Registered Charity No. 48396

Bibliography

A.O.S. – *Ups and Downs of a Blue Coat Boy*
Blue Coat School – *Annual Reports; Minutes*
Cappe, Catherine – *An Account of Two Charity Schools; Memoirs; Origin of Girls' School – Observations*
Cotsworth, Moses B. – *Souvenir of the Bi-Centenary of the York Blue Coat Boys' and Grey Coat Girls' School*
Drake, Francis – *Eboracum*
George, Dorothy M. – *London Life in the Eighteenth Century*
Gray, Mrs Edwin – *Papers and Diaries of a York Family 1764-1839*
Grey Coat School – *Annual Reports; Minutes*
Hargroves, William – *History and Description of the Ancient City of York, 1818 edition*
Jones, M.G. – *The Charity School Movement*
Knight, Charles Brunton – *A History of the City of York*
Knowles – *York Scrapbook 1904-1909*
Murray, Hugh – *Photographs and Photographers of York; Doctor Evelyn's York*
Standing Rules and Orders of the Charity Schools
St Stephen's Home – *Annual Reports; Minutes*
Stacpole A. (ed.) – *The Noble City of York*
Tillot, P.M. (ed.) – *The Victoria County History of Yorkshire, The City of York*
The Yorkshire Evening Press
Torre – *Antiquities*
Trevelyan, G.M. – *English Social History*
Ward, Ann – *The History and Antiquities of the City of York*
York Courant
York Herald
York Oral History Project

Illustration Acknowledgements

Permission to include the following illustrations is gratefully acknowledged:

York Children's Trust	Front cover (*Photograph*: Ken Shelton)
York City Libraries	Frontispiece pp. 2, 3, 19, 25, 26, 50, 53
Miss Doreen Amos	p. 37
Evelyn Collection	pp. 102, 106
Sir Marcus Worsley, Bt.	p. 106
Mrs Monica Peak	p. 111
Mr Peter Gibson MBE, York Glaziers Trust and St Helen's Church	Back cover

Index of People Mentioned

A.O.S., 16
Adams & Co., 23
Amos, C.T.B., 36
Amos, Mrs, 36
Anderson, Lady, 52
Andrews, Cpl., 43
Argles, Miss Helen, 108
Arlidge, Miss Mary, 97, 100, 101
Ashton, James, 40

Barron & Barron, 102
Bazzard, Miss Gladys, 72-84
Beckett, Joseph, 8
Beckwith, Dr Stephen, 17, 61
Beckwith, Wm. Richard, 70
Bedingfield, Mrs, 57
Belfield, Miss, 99
Bilborough, Mrs, 61
Bingley, Lord, 3
Birch, J.P., 86, 88, 91
Birch, W.H., 101
Blencowe, Miss, 95
Bloor, K.W.H., 91
Bloor, Mrs A.M., 87
Body, Canon, 96
Borthwick, William, 46
Bradley, Jean, 86
Bramforth, Mrs, 48
Brierley, Walter, 67
Brittain, Violet, 126
Brotherton, Mr, 109
Brown, Mrs Dorothy, 78

Camidge, John, 49
Cappe, Mrs Catherine, 52-57
Cave, Henry, 10
Cayley, Lady, 121
Cayley, Sir George, 100
Charlton, Leslie, 41
Close, John, 21, 22, 65
Clutton, Frank, 105
Clutton, W.J., 105
Cobb, Sister, 115-125
Coggan, Mrs Jean, 86
Cotsworth, Moses B., 24, 40
Creer, H.L., 41
Cremmett, Mr, 40
Crombie, Ethel, 108

Davies, Robert, 15, 46, 61
Douglas, Rev. J., 95
Drake, Francis, 12
Duncombe, Miss, 97
Duncombe, Mrs, 95

Egerton, Mrs, 95
Eland, Rev. T., 44
Etches, William, 17, 18
Evelyn, Dr W.A., 102, 105, 107, 110

Fairfax, Robert, 3
Farrar, Luke, 50
Fenwick, Hon. Lady, 47
Ferrey, Peter, 92

INDEX OF PEOPLE MENTIONED

Finch, Miss, 64
Finch, Rev. Henry, 2
Ford, John, 20
Foster, L., 39
Fryer, Mr, 79
Fauconberg, Lord, 10

Galtress, Walter, 84
Gent, Thomas, 12
Gill, Alfred, 124
Gill, Canon A.R., 39
Glover, Harry, 42
Gladstone, William, 40
Gowan, Miss, 115
Gray, Miss Elizabeth, 39, 66, 76
Gray, Mrs Faith, 52
Grimthorpe, Lord, 107

Halifax, Viscount, 100
Harcourt, Mrs, 95
Hardy, Canon, 112
Harrison, Barbara J., 125
Harrowell, H.E., 41, 87
Harrowell, Mrs, 87
Haughton, William, 49
Haxby, Thomas, 5
Henry VIII, 3
Herring, Archbishop, 10
Hewley, Lady, 3
Hey, Mrs Daphne, 90, 92, 116
Hildyard, Francis, 10
Hill, David, 20
Hill, J.R., 33
Hooker, Mr, 52
Howard, Catherine, 3
Hudson, George, 15
Hughes, H.C., 27, 34
Hunter, H.L., 24, 27

Jennings, Elizabeth, 73
Jones, John Paul, 9

Kilvington, J., 5

Lawrence, Petty Officer, 43
Leak, Mrs Monica, 127
Leetham, Messrs, 33
Lund, John, 49

Mann, Miss, 97, 101
Marshall, Miss C., 103-114
Mathew, Miss, 95, 96
Mennim, A., 85
Mills, Mrs, 99
Milner, Colonel, 105
Mortimer, Timothy, 8
Morton, H.V., 41
Mungall, Dr D.F., 121

Nelson, Robert, 1
Newcombe, Dr John, 88
Newham, Annabella, 8

O'Loughlin, Mary, 121

Paxton, J.R., 28
Peters, E., 20
Peters, J.A., 20
Phillips, Miss R.H., 101
Prince Albert Victor, 97
Princess Royal, 40
Pulleyn, Creer & Co., 31

Redman, Charles, 2
Rhodes Brown, H., 32, 40, 42
Rhodes Brown, Mrs, 32
Rhodes, Miss O., 28
Richardson, Mrs, 117
Robinson, Edward, 18-24
Robinson, George, 42
Ross, Lucy, 77
Rowntree, Joseph, 15
Rowntree, Messrs, 33

Rymer, A.S., 81
Rymer, E.J., 42

Sanderson, T., 40
Saville, John, 38
Shanks, Miss Ann, 90
Shann, Dr, 20
Shann, Mrs Jane, 66
Shannon, John, 91
Sharp, Dr John, 2
Sharp, Mrs John, 47
Sharp, Robert, 2
Sheriff, Ruth, 121
Sherriff, H.G., 92
Smith, Rev. Sydney, 10
Stableford, Claire, 90-93
Stapylton, Mrs, 111
Steele, W.B., 44
Stephenson, Prof. G., 19
Sterne, Rev. Laurence, 10
Sutcliffe, Herbert, 40
Swainston, Miss, 52
Swann, Robert, 24

Taylor, J.F., 20
Taylor, W.A., 90
Terry, Mrs Frank, 108
Terry, Noel, 117
Thompson, Robert, 93
Thompson, William, 38, 40, 82
Thomson, W.F.H., 105
Thornhill, Frances, 47

Toynbee, Miss, 68
Turner, Miss Alice, 103

Ware, F., 42
Warren, Colonel, 39
Webb, Chris, 38
Webster, E., 85
Wenlock, Baron, 100
West, E.M., 68
Whitwell, George, 40
Wilkinson, Mrs M.E., 91, 93
Wilkinson, Tate, 8
Wilkinson, Thomas, 10
Willson-Pepper, Mrs, 120
Wilson, Miss, 87, 90
Wilson, Alderman, 66
Wolstenholme, Margaret, 48
Wolstenholme, Mr, 49
Worsley, Lady Joyce, 110, 113, 124
Worsley, Miss Katherine, 124
Worsley, Sir William, 110, 111, 113
Worsley, Sir William C., 96, 98, 100
Worsley, Sir William H.A., 100, 109
Worsley, Susan Lady, 101, 109
Wyndham, Colonel George, 105

Yarburgh, Mrs Cooke, 113